Praise for *It's All About the Bike*

"Robert Penn relates his quixotic quest to procure the perfect bicycle with authority and humor, infusing his fluent narrative with thoughtful and provocative digressions that invoke technology, ergonomics, history, and social ideals. He richly deserves his $5,000 'dream machine.'"—**David V. Herlihy, author of *Bicycle: A History* and *The Lost Cyclist: The Epic Tale of an American Adventurer and His Mysterious Disappearance***

"Robert Penn has assembled a splendid patchwork quilt of bicycle history, arcane workshops, and fascinating people into a passionate journey in search of his dream machine. After reading him, you'll never look at a bicycle the same way again and will enjoy riding yours even more. And you'll probably start your own velocipedal quest for perfection into the bargain. A simply lovely excursion not into bicyclists, but into BICYCLES. You must read this before you watch the Tour de France!"—**Brian Fagan, author of *Elixir* and *The Great Warming*, and an avid recreational cyclist with a Penn-like steel framed bike**

"A fantastic new chronicle of the bike's story, from its cultural history to its technical innovation to the fascinating, colorful stories of the people who ride it . . . [Penn] approaches his subject with equal parts humor, humility, and authoritative intelligence as he sets out to find himself a new bike . . . Entertaining, illuminating and beautifully illustrated, *It's All About the Bike* is a rare and precious portal to the heart and soul of bike culture and its surprising footprint—tireprint?—on all of culture."   **—TheAtlantic.com**

"[*It's All About the Bike*] is more than just a gearhead's hejira, a globetrotter's catalog of componentry for the cycling . . . With humor and insight, Penn examines the historical, social, and cultural significance of the bike."
          —*The Philadelphia Inquirer*

"If you've ever felt the wind rolling over your back as you tuck into a downhill or cleared a log with a bunny hop, give [*It's All About the Bike*] a shot. It's a quick read and even serious cyclists will learn something."
          —Associated Press

"The bike is the heart of our cycling lives, but it's a starting point for all sorts of journeys, literal and metaphoric. So Penn's title merits a tiny edit: it's not

It's All About the Bike

The Pursuit of Happiness on Two Wheels

ROBERT PENN

B L O O M S B U R Y

NEW YORK • LONDON • NEW DELHI • SYDNEY

Published by Bloomsbury USA, New York

All papers used by Bloomsbury USA are natural, recyclable products made from
wood grown in well-managed forests. The manufacturing processes conform to
the environmental regulations of the country of origin.

LIBRARY OF CONGRESS CATALOGING-IN-PUBLICATION DATA

Penn, Rob.
It's all about the bike : the pursuit of happiness on two wheels / Robert Penn.
p. cm.
Includes index.
ISBN-13: 978-1-60819-538-1 (hardback)
1. Bicycles. 2. Bicycles—Design and construction. 3. Cycling. I. Title.
TL410.P46 2011
629.227'2—dc22
2010049942

The lines from Patrick Kavanagh's "Inniskeen Road: July Evening"
are reprinted from Collected Poems, edited by Antoinette Quinn
(Allen Lane, 2004), by kind permission of the Trustees of the Estate of the late
Katherine B. Kavanagh, through the Jonathan Williams Literary Agency.

The lines from Seamus Heaney's "A Constable Calls" are reprinted
from New Selected Poems, 1966–1987 by Seamus Heaney,
by kind permission of Faber & Faber.

First published in the UK by Particular Books in 2010
First U.S. Edition published by BloomburyUSA in 2011
This paperback edition published in 2012

Paperback ISBN 978-1-60819-575-6

3 5 7 9 10 8 6 4 2

Typeset by Ellipsis Books Limited, Glasgow
Printed in the U.S.A. by Thomson - Shore, Inc.

Contents

La Petite Reine   1

1 Diamond Soul: The Frame   19
2 Drop Bars, Not Bombs: Steering System   47
3 All Geared Up: Drivetrain   85
4 The Lateral Truth, So Help Me God: Wheels   109
5 On the Rivet: The Saddle   155

Not in Vain the Distance Beckons   177

Selected Reading   187
Appendix: Useful Information   189
Acknowledgements   191
Picture Credits   193
Index   195

ROBERT PENN'S DREAM BIKE

SADDLE

SEATPOST

RIMS

TIRES

FRAME

HANDLEBAR AND STEM

HEADSET

FORKS

PEDALS

HUBS

SPOKES

DRIVETRAIN
(CHAINRINGS, BOTTOM BRACKET,
CRANKS, FREEWHEEL, AND CHAIN)

FRAME: Made to measure, from Reynolds 953 tubing, by Brian Rourke Cycles in Stoke-on-Trent, England: Brian Rourke did the 'fitting' and his son, Jason, welded and painted the frame.

HANDLEBAR AND STEM: From Cinelli in Milan, one of the great marques of Italian road racing componentry established after World War II by Cino Cinelli, a great innovator.

SADDLE: From Brooks in Smethwick, Birmingham: it's based on a model first patented in 1896 and in continuous production ever since. The leather shapes to fit anatomically after 1,500 miles.

WHEELS: The wheels were 'built up' by hand to exact personal specifications by Steve 'Gravy' Gravenites in Fairfax, California.

The components of the wheels were:

RIMS: DT Swiss rims: made of aluminium, with reinforced spoke beds and coated in helicopter rotor paint – very robust.

SPOKES: Made from stainless steel by Sapim in Belgium: the spokes that Lance Armstrong won all seven of his Tours de France on.

HUBS: Made by Royce in Hampshire, a company that exemplifies British engineering excellence.

TIRES: Made largely by hand at Continental in Korbach, Germany, where tire production began in 1892.

DRIVETRAIN: Campagnolo Record, one of the enduring icons of road racing bicycles. Tullio Campagnolo, the founder of the company was a renowned inventor who helped re-style the bicycle in the twentieth century.

FORKS: Made from carbon by Columbus of Milan, one of the great dynasties of Italian cycling.

HEADSET: Made by Chris King Components, Portland, USA: bike jewellery encasing the finest ball bearings a bicycle could wish for.

La Petite Reine

Who climbs with toil, wheresoe'er,
Shall find wings waiting there.

(Henry Charles Beeching, 'Going Down Hill on a Bicycle: A Boy's Song')

'Meet the future,' Butch Cassidy says, showing Etta Place where to sit on the handlebars of his bicycle. By the time B. J. Thomas is singing 'Raindrops Keep Fallin' on My Head' to Burt Bacharach's melancholy tune, Butch and Etta are off, pedalling out of the farmyard down a dusty track.

It's one of the best-known musical interludes in cinema. The song won an Academy Award. When *Butch Cassidy and the Sundance Kid* was released in 1969, the poster featured the pair on the bicycle. For the record, Paul Newman performed the bike tricks himself. The interlude is a pivotal moment in the film: it's not just the law hunting down the ageing gunslingers; the future – symbolized by the bicycle – is chasing them too. As the scene at their farm-hideaway ends, Butch sends the newfangled machine downhill, riderless, into a ditch: 'The future's all yours, you lousy bicycle,' he shouts. Prostrate in the stream, the wheels 'tick, tick, tick' to a halt. Butch and Sundance's time in the West is up. They're off to Bolivia, to try and re-make the past.

William Goldman based his original screenplay – which also

won an Academy Award – on the lives of Robert LeRoy Parker and Harry Longabaugh, a notorious pair of train robbers and members of the Wild Bunch. They fled Wyoming for Argentina in 1901. A period of extraordinary change was over, not only in the Wild West but across the entire Western World.

For many in the 1890s the future came too fast. The decade saw the first international telephone links, the 'scramble for Africa', the foundation of Britain's Labour Party, the rationalization and codification of global sports and the first modern Olympiad. Heroin, radium and radioactivity in uranium were discovered. The Waldorf-Astoria in New York and the Paris Ritz opened. Durkheim invented sociology. Landmarks of social thought included rights for workers and old-age pensions. The Rockefellers and Vanderbilts amassed unprecedented amounts of private wealth. X-rays and cinematography were born. Verdi, Puccini, Tchaikovsky, Mahler, Cézanne, Gauguin, Monet, William Morris, Munch, Rodin, Chekhov, Ibsen, Henry James, W. B. Yeats, Rudyard Kipling, Oscar Wilde, Joseph Conrad and Thomas Hardy were at the height of their creative powers. It was a remarkable decade – the capstone of the Victorian era.

At the heart of it all was the bicycle. In 1890, there were an estimated 150,000 cyclists in the USA: a bicycle cost roughly half the annual salary of a factory worker. By 1895, the cost was a few weeks' wages and there were a million new cyclists each year.

The style of bicycle that Butch and Etta rode was called the 'safety'. It was the first modern bicycle, and the culmination of a long and elusive quest for a human-powered vehicle. It was 'invented' in England in 1885. When the pneumatic tyre was added three years later, making the machine comfortable, the first golden age of the bicycle began. As Victor Hugo wrote: 'An invasion of armies can be resisted, but not an idea whose time has come.' The 'gospel of the wheel' spread so quickly that the masses wondered how something so simple could have remained unknown for so long.

Bicycle manufacturing emerged from its roots as a cottage industry to become big, big business. Bicycles were mass-produced on assembly lines for the first time; the design process was separated from production; specialized factories supplied standardized components. One-third of all patents registered at the US Patent Office in the 1890s were bicycle-related. In fact, the bicycle had its own dedicated patent building in Washington, DC.

At the 1895 Stanley bicycle show in London, the annual industry event, 200 firms displayed 3,000 models. *The Cycle* magazine reported 800,000 bicycles manufactured in Britain that year. Many locksmiths, gunsmiths and anyone with metallurgy skills abandoned their trades and went to work in bicycle factories. In 1896, the peak year for production, 300 firms in the USA made 1.2 million bicycles, making it one of the largest industries in the country. The biggest firm, Columbia, with 2,000 employees at the Hartford works in Connecticut, boasted of making a bicycle a minute.

By the end of the decade, the bicycle had become a utilitarian form of personal transport for millions – the people's nag. For the first time in history, the working class became mobile. As they could now commute, crowded tenements emptied, suburbs expanded and the geography of cities changed. In the countryside, the bicycle helped to widen the gene pool: birth records in Britain from the 1890s show how surnames began to appear far away from the rural locality with which they had been strongly associated for centuries. Everywhere, the bicycle was a catalyst for campaigns to improve roads, literally paving the way for the motor car.

The health benefits of the bicycle met with an appetite for self-improvement that characterized the age: the same workers who pedalled to the factories and the pits founded gymnastic clubs and choirs, libraries and literary societies. At the weekends, they cycled together in clubs. Amateur and professional racing exploded. Cycle racing at tracks or velodromes became the number one American spectator sport. Arthur A. Zimmerman, one of the world's first international sports stars, won over 1,000 races on three continents as an amateur, and then as a pro, including gold medals at the first world cycling championships in Chicago in 1893. In Europe, road racing became hugely popular. Long-lived 'Classic' races such as Liège–Bastogne–Liège and Paris–Roubaix were staged for the first time, in 1892 and 1896 respectively. The Tour de France was inaugurated in 1903.

Americans in particular became captivated by the idea of speed during the Gay '90s: speed was thought to be a mark of civilization. Through transportation and communication, Americans came to associate speed with the unification of their vast country. On a bicycle, they could actualize it. By the end of 1893, track racers surpassed 35 mph. The bicycle eclipsed the trotting horse to become the fastest thing on the road. Technological innovation made the bicycle ever lighter and faster as the decade progressed. In 1891, Monty Holbein set the world 24-hour track record of 577 km (361 miles) at London's Herne Hill velodrome: six years later, the cigar-smoking Dutchman, Mathieu Cordang, rode 400 km (250 miles) further.

A typical bicycle was fixed-wheel (no gears or freewheel), with a steel frame, slightly dropped bars, a leather saddle and usually no brakes (you braked by back-pedalling). Roadsters commonly weighed around 33 lb; racers were under 22 lb – pretty much the weight of the finest road-racing bicycles today. On 30 June 1899, Charles Murphy became the most famous cyclist in America when he rode a mile in 57.45 seconds, paced by a locomotive on the Long Island railroad, on planks laid between the rails.

The bicycle met with the demand of *fin de siècle* society for independence and mobility. The safety introduced whole new groups to two wheels: the old and young (juvenile models were marketed from the early 1890s), the short and the unfit, men and women. For the first time, anyone could ride a bike. Mass production and the burgeoning second-hand market meant that the majority of people could afford one. As the contemporary American author Stephen Crane wrote: 'Everything is bicycle.'

Perhaps the greatest impact of the bicycle was in breaking down hitherto rigid class and gender barriers. There was a democracy to the bicycle that society was powerless to resist. H. G. Wells, described by one biographer as the 'writer laureate of cyclists', used the bicycle in several novels to illustrate the dramatic social changes taking place in Britain. In *The Wheels of Chance*, published at the height of the boom in 1896, the protagonist, Hoopdriver, a lower-middle-class draper's assistant, goes on a cycling holiday and meets a young, upper-middle-class woman who has left home to flaunt 'her freedom – on a bicycle, in country places'. Wells satirizes the British class structure and shows how the bicycle was eroding it. On the road, Hoopdriver and the lady are equals. The dress, clubs, codes, manners and morals that society had put in place to reinforce the existing hierarchy simply didn't exist when one was cycling down a country lane in Sussex.

The novelist John Galsworthy wrote:

The bicycle . . . has been responsible for more movement in manners and morals than anything since Charles the Second . . . Under its influence, wholly or in part, have blossomed weekends, strong nerves, strong legs, strong language . . . equality of sex, good digestion and professional occupation – in four words, the emancipation of women.

The bicycle coincided with, rather than instigated, the feminist movement. It was, nonetheless, a turning point in the long war for women's suffrage. Bicycle manufacturers, of course, wanted women to ride. They had been making ladies' models since the earliest prototype bicycle in 1819. The safety bicycle changed everything, though. Cycling became the first popular athletic pursuit for women. By 1893, nearly every manufacturer was producing a ladies' model.

In September 1893 Tessie Reynolds caused a national sensation when she rode from Brighton to London and back on a man's bicycle, wearing 'rational dress' – a long jacket over a pair of baggy pantaloons cropped and cinched below the knee. It was a turning point in the acceptance of practical clothes for women, most of whom still cycled in voluminous skirts, corsets, petticoats, long-sleeved shirts and jackets with tight neckbands. Later, when the suffragettes' campaign of civil disobedience reached its height in 1912, the incident was seen as a milestone.

MISS LONDONDERRY

In June 1894 Annie London-derry set off from Boston with some spare clothes and a pearl-handled revolver, to cycle round the world. Witty, clever, charismatic – the Becky Sharp of her age – she deliberately took up the mantle of women's equality. She was a paragon of 'New Woman', an American term for the modern woman who behaved as an equal to men. The bicycle, dubbed the 'freedom machine' by historian Robert A. Smith, empowered 'New Woman'.

'The stand she is taking in the matters of dress is no small indication that she has realized that she has an equal right with a man to control her own movements,' Susan B. Anthony said. As the leading suffragette of her day, and the woman who gained fame when she was arrested for voting in the 1872 presidential election, she knew. In an interview in the *New York Sunday World* in 1896, she said:

Let me tell you what I think of bicycling. I think it has done more to emancipate women than anything else in the world . . . It gives a woman a feeling of freedom and self-reliance . . . the moment she takes her seat, she knows she can't get into harm unless she gets off her bicycle, and away she goes, the picture of free, untrammelled womanhood.

By the time Butch and Sundance were bound for South America, the bicycle had won broad social acceptance and struck deep into the nexus of society. In a decade, cycling had evolved from a faddish leisure pursuit, exclusive to a tiny minority of wealthy athletic males, to become the most popular form of transport on the planet. It still is today.

The bicycle is one of mankind's greatest inventions – it's up there with the printing press, the electric motor, the telephone, penicillin and the World Wide Web. Our ancestors thought it one of their greatest achievements. This idea is now coming back into fashion. The cultural status of the bicycle is rising again. The machine is becoming more embedded in Western society, through urban infrastructure design, transport policy, environmental concerns, the profile of cycle sport and leisure practices. In fact, there is a whisper that we might today be at the dawn of a new golden age of the bicycle.

★

The bicycle can be described in under fifty words: a steerable machine comprising two wheels with pneumatic tyres, mounted in-line on a frame with rotating front forks, propelled by the rider's feet turning pedals attached by cranks to a chainwheel, and by a loop of chain to sprockets on the rear wheel. It's very simple. The bicycle can be ridden, on a reasonable surface, at four or five times the pace of walking, with the same amount of effort – making it the most efficient, self-powered means of transportation ever invented. Fortunately learning to ride a bicycle is easy (so easy, in fact, that many of our primate cousins have got the hang of it too). And, once learnt, riding a bicycle is something we never forget.

I've ridden a bike most days of my adult life. I can't, though, remember the first time I rode a bike as a child. I know I'm supposed to. I'm supposed to recall perfectly that moment of epiphany we've all shared, when the stabilizers were removed on an incline in the local park; when the hand of my father pulled back and I wobbled forward into the great equilibrium that I will never leave; the moment when I unconsciously steered, albeit unsteadily, the support points of the bicycle under the centre of mass, and first grasped the esoteric principle – balance. But no, I'm afraid I can't remember it. In fact, I can't even remember my first bike.

The first bike I can remember was a purple Raleigh Tomahawk, the diminutive version of the Chopper. I progressed to a Raleigh Hustler: purple again, and pimped up with white handlebar tape, a white saddle, a white water bottle, white cable guides and white tyres — it was the '70s. When I outgrew this, Grandma stepped in with a fifth-hand, Dawes three-speed, kids' roadster. Compared to the Hustler, it had the panache of coveralls, but it flew. During the summer of 1978 I rode loops of my neighbourhood from dawn to dusk. My parents saw I'd got the bike-bug. The following spring, I was given a ten-speed Viking racer — a black thoroughbred. It was in the window of the local bike shop when I went to collect it. 'Ever bike?' Jack London wrote. 'Now that's something that makes life worth living! . . . Oh, to just grip your handlebars and lay down to it, and go ripping and tearing through streets and road, over railroad tracks and bridges, threading crowds . . . and wondering all the time when you're going to smash up. Well, now, that's something!' That's how I felt on my Viking racer. I was born restless. Aged 12, I finally had wings.

When I landed, I was a teenager. The bug — to ride and ride, for the sheer love of it — had gone. I abandoned the rhythmic cadence of two wheels for the rhythmic sounds of 'Two Tone'. Of course, I still used a bike to get around: three unloved, beat-up racers followed. At the beginning of my final year at university, my flatmate arrived on a red tandem. We did moonlit time trials round the Georgian squares. The bike was so honest and so red; we named it — Otis.

In 1990, I bought my first mountain bike — a no-nonsense, British-built, rigid Saracen Sahara. I rode it from Kashgar in China to Peshawar in Pakistan, over the Karakoram mountains and the Hindu Kush. When I was back in London, working as a lawyer, the Saracen more than carried me around: it represented life beyond the pinstripe suits. Then it got stolen. A succession of mountain bikes, customized for commuting, followed: a Kona Lava Dome, two Specialized Stumpjumpers, a Kona Explosif and others. They all got stolen. I once had two stolen in a weekend. There were excursions along the Ridgeway, and to Dartmoor

and the Lake District, but most of the time these bikes merely conveyed me across the city's backside.

On a wintry Saturday afternoon in 1995, I walked into Roberts Cycles, a venerated frame builder in South London, and ordered a bespoke touring frame. It was called 'Mannanan', after the mythical Celtic figure Mannanan mac Lir, who protects the Isle of Man, where I grew up. I cycled across the USA, Australia, South-East Asia, the Indian subcontinent, Central Asia, the Middle East and Europe – effectively around the world. The American bike mechanic, Lennard Zinn wrote: 'Be at one with the universe. If you can't do that, at least be at one with your bike.' After three years and 25,000 miles, I was.

Today, Mannanan is on the wall in my shed. I own five other bikes: a ten-year-old, steel Specialized Rockhopper, which I am continually rebuilding to keep it in serviceable, commuting order. My old road bike, for winter riding, is a hotchpotch of componentry on a Nervex aluminium frame with Ambrosio carbon forks. The new road bike is a Wilier, with a sleek, Italian-designed carbon frame, manufactured in Taiwan. My old mountain bike is a Schwinn. My new mountain bike is the most recent purchase: a super-light Felt aluminium, cross-country hard tail, perfect for the trails in the Brecon Beacons, where I now live and ride.

With this small troop of hard-working bicycles, my bases are covered. Yet something fundamental is missing. Like tens of thousands of everyday cyclists with utilitarian machines, I recognize there is a glaring hole in my bike shed, a cavernous space for something else, something special. I'm in the middle of a lifelong affair with the bicycle: none of my bikes even hints at this.

I've been riding bicycles for thirty-six years. Today, I ride to get to work, sometimes for work, to keep fit, to bathe in air and sunshine, to go shopping, to escape when the world is breaking my balls, to savour the physical and emotional fellowship of riding with friends, to travel, to stay sane, to skip bathtime with my kids, for fun, for a moment of grace, occasionally to impress someone, to scare myself and to hear my boy laugh. Sometimes I ride my bicycle just to ride my bicycle. It's a broad church of practical, physical and emotional reasons with one unifying thing – the bicycle.

I need a new bike. I could go on-line right now with a credit card and spend $5,000 on a mass-produced carbon or titanium racing bike. I could be tanking through the hills on a superb new machine at sunset tomorrow. It's tempting, very tempting. But it's not right. Like many people, I'm frustrated at the round of buying stuff that is designed to be replaced quickly. I want to break the loop with this bike. I'm going to ride it for thirty years or more and I want to savour the process of acquiring it. I want the best bike I can afford, and I want to grow old with it. Besides, I'm only going to spend this kind of money once. I require more than a good bike. In fact, I require a bike you can't buy on the Internet; a bike you can't buy anywhere. Anyone who rides a bike regularly and has even the faintest feeling of respect or

ON TOUR: TRACING THE DAY'S ITINERARY.

affection for their own steed will know this hankering – I want *my* bike.

I need a talismanic machine that somehow reflects my cycling history and carries my cycling aspirations. I want craftsmanship, not technology; I want the bike to be man-made; I want a bike that has character, a bike that will never be last year's model. I want a bike that shows my appreciation of the tradition, lore and beauty of bicycles. The French nickname for the bicycle is *La Petite Reine* – I want my own 'little queen'.

I know where to start. The bicycle frame will be made to measure and hand-built by an artisan frame-builder. Few people know this, but you can have a custom-built frame, designed to fit your body and tuned for the type of riding you do, for a lot less money than many exotic, mass-manufactured stock frames sold in shops. Sixty years ago, every large town in northern Italy, France, Belgium and Holland would have had at least one frame-builder. In Britain, where the concentration was greatest, big cities had dozens. While a handful of giant manufacturers such as Rudge-Whitworth, Raleigh and BSA in Britain, Bianchi in Italy and Peugeot in France catered for the cycling masses, small frame-builders built bikes for clubmen, racers, touring cyclists and the cognoscenti. These craftsmen made a few dozen frames a year, with great attention to detail and individual flourishes. Tim Hilton, in his loving memoir of the post-war cycling scene, *One More Kilometre and We're in the Showers*, called these hand-built frames 'industrial folk art'. The simple tools – files, hacksaws, blowtorches and a device to hold the tubes while brazing – rooted the frame-builders in an innovative, artisan culture that dated back to the beginning of bicycle manufacturing. Even Raleigh started as a small workshop, making three bicycles a week in 1888.

By 1951, Raleigh was making 20,000 a week. The early 1950s were dizzy heights for the bicycle industry in Europe. There were 12 million regular cyclists in Britain alone. As the major manufacturers boomed, so did the small-town frame-builders. Collectors now only remember their names – Major Nichols and Ron Cooper in Britain, Alex Singer and René Herse in France, Faliero Masi and Francesco Galmozzi in Italy, to name just a handful from the hundreds.

Up to the end of the 1950s, the bicycle was still the main form of utility transport for working people across Europe. In Britain, cycling was also the major leisure activity. The cities emptied of young people at the weekends. The British countryside, already over-imagined by advertisers and authors, filled to bursting with eager cyclists in pursuit of bucolic bliss.

The car was coming, though. The 3.5 million bikes sold in Britain in 1955 had dropped to 2 million by 1958. The Mini went on sale in 1959. Small frame-builders began to disappear. There was a brief revival in the 1970s, when the oil crisis created an explosion of demand in the USA. For a few years, the Americans couldn't get their hands on British and Italian lightweight racing frames fast enough. Spellbound young men crossed the Atlantic to learn frame-building in London and Milan. Richard Sachs, Ben Serotta and Peter Weigle – a sort of holy trinity of American frame-builders today – all apprenticed at the once renowned Witcomb Cycles in Deptford, south-east London, in the 1970s.

By the mid-seventies, the cultural perception of the bicycle had reached a low point in Britain. It was no longer seen as a valid form of transportation: it was a toy, or worse – a pest. This view

is only seriously being revised today. When I was working as a
lawyer in London in the early 1990s, I commuted to work by
bicycle. Most people thought I was, at best, odd. I used to ride
through Hyde Park every day: I knew most of the other bike
commuters by Christian name, as there were so few of us. There
was an overt sense of cyclists versus motorists on the city streets.
The monthly Critical Mass rides were practically anarchist events,
often involving rolling battles with the police. The heroin-chic
cycle couriers were the flag carriers: they knifed through static
traffic, surfing the tiny gaps, high on car fumes and the smell of
seething motorists.

The bike shop I used near Holborn was a favourite of this
warrior-courier class. One Friday night I dropped in after work,
to pick up my bike. I had sheared off one of the cranks. The
mechanic wheeled the bike out of the workshop, past three
couriers sharing a can of Tennent's Extra. The old crank, a lump
of aluminium, was strapped to my handlebar with a round of tape.

'What's that for?' I said, pointing at the old crank. I looked at
the mechanic who looked at the couriers, who looked at the
mechanic, who looked at me. Clearly I was supposed to know
what it was for, even if I was standing there in a grey pinstripe
suit. After a long pause, the middle courier looked at me with
wild eyes and said: 'You . . . stick . . . it . . . through . . . the . . .
windscreen . . . of . . . a . . . fucking . . . car!'

Moving to the Brecon Beacons in Wales seven years ago was
another eye-opener in the cultural perception of the bicycle. In
the city, there was at least, by then, a growing body of people
who acknowledged the health and transport benefits of riding a
bicycle. In the countryside, you only rode a bike if you'd lost
your driving licence. For a Welsh hill farmer there could be no
other reason. Period. The locals watched me pedal in and out of
Abergavenny every day, and wondered.

Five months after moving in, I was in the local pub, high up on a hillside, on a Friday night. An old boy I knew only by the name of his farm, cupped my elbow and led me gently to a corner of the bar. He fixed me with a stern gaze: 'I see yor on the bike,' he said. 'How long you lost your licence for then, boy?' I explained that I hadn't lost my licence; that I chose to ride a bicycle every day because, well, I just loved it. He winked at me and tapped a gnarled finger on his wind-dried nose. A year later, the farmer again took me aside in the pub, on a Friday night. This time the gaze was even sterner. 'I see yor on the bike still, boy,' he said. 'A long time to be banned now, see. You can tell me . . . did you daw something tehr-ribble in a car? Did you kill a child?'

The very best artisan frame-builders have more in common with the craftsmen who make Patek Philippe watches, Monteleone guitars or Borelli shirts than with the mass manufacturers who churn out carbon and aluminium frames from factories in the Far East. Not long ago, much of what we owned was alive with the skill, and even the idealism, of the people who made it – the blacksmith who forged our tools, the cobbler, the wood-turner, the carpenter, the wheelwright, and the seamstress and tailor who made the clothes we wore. We retain possessions that are well made; over time, they grow in value to us, and enrich our lives when we use them. The frame is the soul of the bicycle. The frame of my bike will only be made once, from steel.

The bike will look like a racing bike, but it will be finely tuned to meet my cycling needs. If you like, it will be a 'riding' bike. I'm not going to race, but I'll ride this bike regularly and I'll ride it fast. I'll ride it round the Brecon Beacons and across Britain. I'll ride 'centuries' with my friends and cyclosportives. I'll ride it the length of the Pyrenees, over the Col du Galibier, up Mont Ventoux and down the Pacific Coast Highway. When I'm feeling blue, I'll ride it to work. And when I'm 70, no doubt I'll ride it to the pub.

The components – the handlebar, stem, forks, headset, hubs, rims, spokes, bottom bracket, freewheel, chainwheel, sprockets, chain, derailleurs, cranks, brakes, pedals and saddle – will be chosen to match the frame. They won't be the lightest or the sexiest components on the market. They'll simply be the best made. The wheels will be built by hand. I'll visit workshops and factories in Italy, America, Germany and Britain to see all the components I want on my bike being made. Individually, each component will be something special; collectively, they'll make my dream bike.

The bicycle saves my life every day. If you've ever experienced a moment of awe or freedom on a bicycle; if you've ever taken flight from sadness to the rhythm of two spinning wheels, or felt the resurgence of hope pedalling to the top of a hill with the dew of effort on your forehead; if you've ever wondered, swooping bird-like down a long hill on a bicycle, if the world was standing still; if you have ever, just once, sat on a bicycle with a singing heart and felt like an ordinary human touching the gods, then we share something fundamental. We know it's all about the bike.

1. Diamond Soul

The Frame

Handing over a bank note is enough to make a bicycle belong to me,
but my entire life is needed to realize this possession.

(Jean-Paul Sartre)

'Well, you don't look like a complete bag o' rags,' Brian Rourke
said, in his soft Potteries burr. He was standing back, with one
hand clamped on his chin and the other upturned on his hip,
looking at me astride my bike. Lithe, energetic and refusing to
acknowledge his seventy years, he was a good advert for a life
spent cycling. 'Jump off the bike now while I fetch a few things.'

Brian Rourke Cycles occupies a converted squash centre in
Stoke-on-Trent. Downstairs is a smart retail bike shop. Upstairs,
the old bar has been transformed into Brian's office, where he
carries out all the bike fittings. It is a shrine to the sport of road
cycle racing. There is a wall of framed bike magazine covers,
with riders on Rourke frames leading races; there are photos of
Merckx, Gimondi, Kelly and other giants of the sport; iconic
Tour de France images; Mario Cipollini's actual 1998 Tour de
France bike; a row of silver cups and other pieces of arcane
memorabilia. To the right of the door is a merino wool World
Champion's jersey worn by Tommy Simpson, the lionhearted
anti-hero of British cycling who collapsed and died with drugs

and alcohol in his blood during the Tour de France in raging 113°F heat on 13 July 1967.

On the opposite wall is a photo of Brian beside Nicole Cooke, the outstanding British road cyclist and Olympic champion: 'She's been coming into the shop since she was 12,' Brian said. 'Won four world junior championships on Rourke frames. Wonderful girl.' Less prominent is a photo of Brian as a younger man, tilting into a corner, gripping the handlebars, staring ahead, looking hungry, racing hard.

'Yes, yes, I raced a bit,' he said, bustling back into the room. Actually, he raced a lot. In his prime, he rode for the Great Britain team in three Milk Races and was National Champion. Carlton and Falcon both offered him a professional contract but there was no money in it then. 'I packed it in, in 1967. Pity, really, but I can't complain.' Racing's loss was the frame-building industry's gain: Brian has been designing and fitting customers to hand-built bicycles almost ever since. In that time, he has never run out of orders for his bespoke bikes. I estimated he must have been through the fitting process some 5,000 times.

Frame-builders from the golden age of British bespoke bicycles in the mid-twentieth century, men like Harry Quinn of Liverpool and Jack Taylor from Stockton-on-Tees, could, I'd been told, size you up as you walked through the door of the workshop. Their experience was such that they needed just one look at you to know the dimensions of the frame you required.

A more reliable fitting or sizing method dating from that time and still popular now is to take body measurements and interpret them into a frame size. Inside leg (crotch to floor), torso, arm, femur, forearm, shoulder width, shoe-size, height and weight all go into the analysis. In this way, the experience of the person doing the fitting and designing of the frame is, again, crucial.

Today, for both professional athletes and amateur riders with deep pockets, there are various high-tech fitting methods that entail a scientific approach to the biomechanics of cycling. They involve motion capture systems that process data taken from anatomical points on a rider, providing a real-time view of the riding position and pedal action at different workloads. The rider being fitted usually sits on an adjustable jig or 'size-cycle', a simple frame mounted on a machine that provides traction when you pedal.

Of course, for the majority of people, buying a bicycle involves a 'fitting process' that is over in under fifteen minutes: the man in the local bike shop sits you on three different bikes, one after the other, takes your credit card while you pedal once round the block; you return and pay. Job done.

Brian's fitting method is different; it's what first drew me to him. There are no more than a handful of frame-builders left in Britain: perhaps a dozen businesses and another dozen hobbyists. On a wet weekend in March, I'd set off to visit as many of them as I could. I criss-crossed the country from Bristol to Bradford via Derby, Leeds, Sheffield and Manchester. In the garage of a suburban semi, I watched Lee Cooper fabricating elegant steel frames for the London fixed-wheel market. Neil Orrell showed me one of his distinctively designed track frames, and photos of a bike he'd once built for a 7-foot man. At Pennine Cycles, Paul Corcoran told me how the shop's founder, Johnny Mapplebeck, had fallen in love with Italian racing bikes when with the Eighth Army during the Allied campaign in Italy. When he was discharged, he began making frames with names like *Scelta dei Campioni* ('Choice of Champions') and *Re della corsa* ('King of the Race'), names that must have sounded exotic in post-war Yorkshire. At Bob Jackson Cycles in Leeds, frames were being boxed to ship to America. I met the ebullient owner, Donald Thomas. He liked his Bob Jackson bicycle so much that he bought the company.

At Mercian Cycles, where three frame-builders work full-time in a workshop that can't have changed in half a century, Grant Mosley told me how the clientele *had* changed: 'They were all club lads when I started. Following the decline in the 1970s, it was just the diehards – you know, the socks, sandals and beards brigade. Today, it's young professional people.'

It was a delightful journey, fuelled by innumerable mugs of tea. Everywhere I saw pride in workmanship, and a connection to the tradition of British craftsmanship that has set standards worldwide for a century. I would have been happy to have a bike from all of them, but as I was after only *one* bike, I picked Brian Rourke Cycles.

It was easy to justify. Brian was a racer, not only as a young man but also as a 'veteran'. In fact, he'd won the National Vets Championship aged 40 and again at 50. Racing bikes are in his blood. I wanted a racing bike. Jason, Brian's son and the man who would weld my frame, had a knowledge and passion that was clear. I liked the lads who worked in the shop. I thought not only will I get the most exquisitely built frame, but the process of being fitted, watching it being made and painted, and then having the bike assembled at Rourke Cycles, would be good fun. Above all, Brian's experience fitting people to bicycles and designing frames is unequalled.

Brian likes his customers to bring their current bike into the shop. He then adjusts or 'sets up' this bike so they are 'bang on' the right position. Often, customers are sent away to ride the new set-up, to ensure it's comfortable. When everyone is happy, measurements are taken from the bike, as the guide, and Brian designs the new frame. It's simple and practical. It relies heavily on his experience. 'Some customers, they just want to give me the dimensions of their existing bike down the phone and have us build a bike. I won't do that. Who's to say they haven't been riding the wrong bike for years? I like to have a good look at everyone first,' he said.

In the two hours I'd been in the shop, Brian had raised the saddle of my Wilier racing bike by tiny increments, three or four times, and shifted it back a centimetre on its rails; he'd replaced the handlebar stem for one 20 mm longer; finally, he exchanged my handlebar for a new one – a classic shaped bar with small 'D' loops, 'so your hands can reach the brake levers more easily,' he said. In that time, my position on the bike had changed significantly. I could feel it. My back was straighter. My weight was more evenly distributed. The new position felt more aerodynamic, more aggressive and, perhaps surprisingly, more comfortable. The bike looked better too: the longer stem and the new handlebar somehow made the machine look better proportioned. It was like placing a painting in the right frame, I thought.

The methodology behind the fitting process was simple enough: 'Bum, hands, feet – three contact points with the bike,' Brian said. First he got my saddle height exactly right. Then he adjusted the saddle backwards, to get me in a position to obtain the maximum leverage from the pedals. Finally, he worked on my hands.

Standing back again, dropping his long metal ruler to the floor and scribbling some notes, Brian said: 'You were a bit stuck on the bike before, plonked there like a brick. That's looking good now. Take the bike away. Come back in a month and we'll go for a ride together. I'll want to know how it feels. If you're going to have a handmade bike, you want it to be yours, don't you? It's got to be exactly the right fit, right for you, not for anyone else.'

This goes to the heart of why anyone would want a hand-built bike: it will fit perfectly, like a bespoke suit from Savile Row. There are several other significant advantages – with the benefit of expert advice, you get to choose the ideal frame tubing diameters, wall thickness and butting lengths, which will fine tune the feel of the bike; importantly, you get a frame designed for the type of cycling you propose to do, where you propose to do it and even your riding style; you get to select the best components you can afford and the colour the frame will be painted; also, you get to savour the process of acquiring the frame; lastly, when the bike is complete and you're out on the road, the machine will turn heads. But really, it's all about having a bike that fits *you* perfectly, a bike that will provide years of pain-free cycling. Most large bike manufacturers produce between five and eight different sizes in each model of bike. The human race doesn't come in five, or even eight sizes.

To make his point, Brian had wheeled his own racing bike into the room. The frame was built by Jason. It was a beautiful bike, of course, but something significant happened when Brian jumped on to it, catching his weight on the pedals and his shoulder against the wall. The bike changed. It fitted Brian so perfectly that it came alive. It responded to his every move, as he shifted his hands briskly around the handlebars and transferred his weight back and forth.

Perhaps more surprising was that Brian changed too. Jumping on to the bike took thirty years off him. When he thrust his hands into the 'D' of the handlebars and sunk his torso across the top tube, his eyes flamed. He was ready to chase down a breakaway from the peloton in a race or launch a sprint for the finishing line.

Just sitting on the bike, just being on his immaculate, bespoke bicycle summoned such powerful emotional memories that three decades of toil and wear were erased from his demeanour in a trice. The bike was a source of youthfulness and it was thrilling to witness.

But that wasn't the point. The point was made when Brian stepped off the bike, swung it round and wheeled it across to me. It was breathtakingly light, well balanced and delightful to hold in my fingers. But when I hopped on to it as Brian had done, there was no transformation. It didn't look special under me. I didn't feel special on top of it. Although Brian and I are the same height and roughly the same weight, we are physically different in many other ways. Our arm, torso, shoulder, leg and thigh measurements are unlikely to be the same. It was Brian's bike: it made me want my own more than ever.

There is a simple grace about an unadorned bicycle frame. Looking at the row of bare, handmade frames hanging on the wall of Brian's shop, something struck me: though they were all made from different types of tubing, painted to individual specifications with different dimensions and angles, and would be built up into different types of bicycle and ridden in very different ways over varied terrain by diverse humans, they were all – in one fundamental way – alike. The frames were all the same shape: diamond.

The first diamond-shaped frame bicycle – the Rover Safety – was manufactured in 1885, in the unloved city of Coventry. It was called the 'safety' because the wheels were the same size and small, the rider's centre of gravity was over the centre of the bike, and he or she could touch the ground with both feet: in short, it was safe to ride. It was the first modern bicycle – something we'd recognize and be able to pedal today.

The 'inventor', John Kemp Starley, later said in a speech to the
Royal Society of Arts:

The main principles which guided me in making this machine were to
place the rider at the proper distance from the ground . . . to place the
seat in the right position in relation to the pedals . . . to place
the handles in such a position in relation to the seat that the rider could
exert the greatest force upon the pedals with the least amount of fatigue.

It was almost exactly what Brian had been saying to me all
morning. Where a rider's hands, feet and backside are placed on
a bicycle for maximum efficiency, control and comfort is a matter
of basic ergonomics, which has been essentially unchanged over
a century.

These principles led Starley
to design the lightest, strongest, cheapest, most rigid, most
compact and ergonomically
most efficient shape the bicycle frame could be. By 1890,
'every maker worthy of the
name' in Coventry, Birming-
ham and Nottingham was producing a safety model. The safety
swept away every type of bicycle that preceded it: velocipedes,
high-wheelers, dwarf ordinaries, the Facile, the Kangaroo,
tricycles, tandem tricycles and quadricycles were obsolete within
a few years. The ultimate form of the bicycle had arrived.

Other safety-style bicycles were designed and patented before
the Rover, but making the bicycle user-friendly animated Starley:
his design was the best. He was also a good businessman and
recognized the potential in the machine early on. In 1889, he
adopted limited liability. In 1896, he floated J. K. Starley & Co

as the Rover Cycle Company. The capital financed the construction of the largest cycle works in Coventry, then the global centre of bicycle manufacturing, and enabled him to survive the first big downturn in the industry at the end of the 1890s.

In 1904, Rover moved into car manufacturing, which was so profitable, so quickly, that the company dropped the bicycle arm of the business altogether. Starley himself had died suddenly in 1901, aged 46. Every cycle firm in Coventry closed their works on the day of his funeral, which was attended by 20,000 people.

Perhaps the mourners had the prescience to know the Rover Safety was a transport phenomenon, and that the basic shape of the bicycle would remain unchanged for the whole of the twentieth century. Contrast the Wright Flyer, the world's first powered aircraft built by Wilbur and Orville Wright (both bike mechanics, as it happens) in 1903, with, say, Concorde. Or take Karl Benz's four-stroke vehicle powered by a gasoline engine, also invented in 1885, and compare it to a contemporary Formula 1 racing car.

In both modes of transport, aeroplane and motor car, the vehicles have changed almost continuously. With the Rover Safety, however, the modern bicycle arrived virtually perfectly formed. Today in aeroplanes and automobiles and countless other mechanical devices there are numerous design variations and opportunities for improvement. With the bicycle, there is one absolute shape. Sir Isaac Newton said we make advances by standing on the shoulders of giants. No one has been able to climb upon Starley's back.

I've had nineteen bikes. This number includes neither bikes that I've owned for less than a month, nor the bikes I've never bothered to lock up. Out of those nineteen bikes, eighteen were built according to the principles of the Safety. The only exception was my Raleigh Tomahawk. The 'ape-hanger', hi-rise handlebars, different-sized wheels, odd-shaped frame and spongy saddle with backrest may have been as cool as the Lone Ranger, but riding a Tomahawk was like pedalling through molasses, dragging a dead pig. Like its big cousin, the Chopper, the Tomahawk was designed in response to the dirt-track roadster bikes popular in the USA in the late 1960s. For the manufacturer, Raleigh, the Chopper opened up a new market in children's bikes, and it marked a shift in the company's philosophy; the bicycle became a consumer goods product, rather than a valid form of transportation. Though remembered fondly, the Chopper was a toy, not a bicycle. It's the worst example of the collapse in confidence in the real value of the bicycle that happened in the 1970s.

The principal structural function of the bicycle frame is to 'maintain integrity' under loads, to have the strength and rigidity to hold the wheels in place and support the rider, and to absorb the rider's efforts in pedalling, braking and steering, as the machine rolls forward. The triangulated, tubular diamond frame remains the best structure to do this. An architect or engineer would describe it as a 'truss structure': the diamond frame is a variation on the super-strong 'seven-membered' truss, a common element in structural and mechanical engineering. Trusses on the roofs of buildings apply the same principles.

There have been hundreds, perhaps thousands of attempts to better the diamond frame design in the century and a quarter since it 'set the fashion to the world'. None could be said to have got close. There have been innumerable refinements in the materials used to make frames, and the constructional aspects of bicycle tubing – non-round shapes, varying wall thicknesses, and tapered diameters – have become highly sophisticated. But the basic diamond shape, made up of two triangles, remains unchanged. Racing, mountain, touring, hybrid, track, utility, cruiser, fixed-wheel, dirt-jumper, porteur and BMX – almost all bicycles are constructed with a diamond frame. Today, the global fleet numbers well over a billion: nearly every one is made to Starley's paradigm. You can spend $15 on a rusting roadster at a yard sale, or $120,000 on a 24-carat gold-plated bicycle encrusted with Swarovski crystals, and you'll still get a diamond frame.

The constant shape of the bicycle over the last century goes some way to explaining why, today, we find riding one so elementary. It's also why there is a sense of classical moderation in the kind of pleasure cycling offers. As the late Sheldon Brown, the esteemed bike mechanic wrote: The diamond frame 'is one of the most nearly perfect pieces of design known, due to . . . its purity of form'.

When I rang Brian, a month after my initial fitting in the shop, to arrange our ride, he immediately asked: 'How's that bike?' I had ridden it daily and it was very comfortable. He recalled all the adjustments he'd made, even though he must have worked on hundreds of bikes in the intervening weeks. Only after I'd commented on each of them to his satisfaction did he ask how I was.

We met up a few miles north-east of Stoke-on-Trent, on the moors, and rode along a ridge with grand views towards the Peak District. Brian knew every geographical feature in sight: this is where he trained when he was racing. He pointed to distant hills and described riding up them on single-speed bicycles; he recounted descents into steep-sided valleys on bleak days in forgotten winters, with failing brakes. Together, the stories created an alternative map of the area, with a distinct narrative. I remembered an Ernest Hemingway quote: 'It is by riding a bicycle that you learn the contours of a country best, since you have to sweat up the hills and coast down them . . . you have no such accurate remembrance of country you have driven through.'

Brian rode beside or behind me, examining my pedal cadence and analysing my position on the bike in different circum-stances – accelerating, climbing, 'watching the cows', descending and sprinting. We didn't go far. It was grey and the wind was scudding across the tops of the hills.

'I've had a good look at you,' Brian said. 'Back to the shop, then?'

There were a couple more incremental adjustments – saddle height again and the position of the brake hoods on the handle-bars – before Brian got out his long metal ruler and started noting down the measurements of my frame in his notepad. Down on his knees, with the ruler pressed against the head tube and the seat post, he asked, 'What's this frame going to be made of then, Rob?'

There were few sure things about this bicycle at the outset, but one of them was the frame material: steel. It's been the backbone of the bicycle for over a century. Until the mid-1970s, it was the only real option. Even in the early 1990s, the majority of high-quality bikes still had steel frames. Today there are many materials on the market: aluminium, titanium and carbon-fibre-reinforced polymers are common, but you might prefer your personalized steed to be made from moulded plastic, magnesium, beryllium (a toxic chemical element found in minerals and used in rocket nozzles), hemp, wood and bamboo. In fact, bamboo is emerging as the new material of choice for socially entrepreneurial frame-building projects in Africa, though it was first used to make bicycles a century ago.

I've tried all the major frame materials. I've had aluminium road bikes with carbon forks, steel mountain bikes, aluminium mountain bikes, a steel touring bike, a titanium road bike, a full-carbon road bike and an aluminium mountain bike with carbon seat stays. So which material, or combination, provides the best overall ride? I have my opinions on all the bikes I've had but I know they are affected by my personal experiences riding them: how long I had the bike, where I rode it, who I rode with. Objectively, I'd be pushed to say which material provides the best overall ride. I know from reading about it that frame materials do have different properties: in fact, some people eulogize profusely about the 'ride characteristics' of this material over that. I'm not so sure. Such things are very subtle, and only measurable with sensitive engineering instruments.

There is much nonsense passing as wisdom about materials for bike frames. The reality is that a good bike builder can make a good frame out of any of the materials mentioned, with any desired ride qualities: if the diameter of the tubes, the thickness of the tube walls and the geometry of the frame are right, the bike will be right.

The poppycock really piles up when people talk about the *stiffness* of a particular frame material: this property of a material is measured by something called Young's *modulus* or *elastic modulus*.

A *stiff* frame transmits the impact of every pebble and nick in the tarmac directly to the nerves in your gluteus maximus, that is, your bum, while a *flexible* frame absorbs the shocks. Most people who have ridden both aluminium and steel frames would say that aluminium frames are stiffer. Actually, steel has a much higher Young's *modulus* than aluminium – it is stiffer. It's just that aluminium tubes tend to be much larger in diameter than steel, and as a tube's diameter increases, its stiffness increases to the third power of that number.

In reality, the tyres, the wheels, the seat posts and the saddle proper absorb the bumps. The frame itself contributes little or nothing to shock absorbency. It's also important to remember that two frames made from different materials would not be made to the same tubing dimensions, making a relative comparison impossible. The frame feature that does have some bearing on comfort is the design of the rear triangle – the triangle formed by the seat post tube, the chain stays and the seat stays.

The most deceptive aspect of modern bike frames is weight. The frame of my newest road bike is carbon (Toray T-700 SC carbon, if you must know). It weighs under 3.5 lb. It's 'Phwoarrr'-light. People who aren't familiar with modern road-racing bicycles pick it up and actually go, 'Phwoarrr'. Unquestionably, the lighter a bike is, the easier it is to pedal uphill. But the industry has become obsessed with making bikes lighter when, for the vast majority of riders, the paramount consideration is not weight, but that a frame should not break in use.

Carbon fibre is currently the most popular frame material for elite professionals, largely because it is so light. If your absolute priority is having the lightest bike possible, because you're a professional cyclist and you need to shave seconds off the time it takes you to climb a 12 mile mountain road in the Pyrenees, to give you a competitive advantage, make a living and put food on the table for your children, then you must have a carbon frame. For the rest of us, it's either an indulgence or we're victims of a conspiracy. Or both.

Yes, even the bicycle industry has a conspiracy theory. It goes like this: the manufacturers of mass-produced bicycles spend a fortune on R&D to ensure that the top professionals they sponsor ride the lightest, fastest bicycles, and win races. The manufacturers need to recoup this expenditure while reducing the costs of production, so they throw everything at marketing to the public the same, or similar, elite bikes as the pros ride.

My dream bicycle will be made from steel. Here's why:

1. Steel is very strong. High-quality steel has a very high *yield strength* or *elastic range* – the point at which it bends permanently rather than bends back to its original shape – making it durable and less likely to bend in a crash. This means that steel tubes can be thin, with a small diameter, making steel frames light and sufficiently flexible. As people like to say: 'steel is real'.

2. Steel has a long life. When I visited Argos Cycles, a well-established frame-building workshop on an industrial estate in Bristol, I was shown several dozen steel frames dating back to World War II. There were frames made by some of the great names, such as Hetchins and A. S. Gillott, hanging on the wall, awaiting restoration work. They were about to be realigned, shot-blasted, rubbed down, primed and resprayed. Further along the wall there were several fully restored, gleaming frames waiting to be collected. They looked brand new. 'Years of riding left in them,' Mark, the workshop manager, told me. 'We have a near constant supply of steel frames in for restoration. Many are over fifty years old. A carbon frame simply won't last anything like that long.'

3. Steel is not prone to sudden failure: despite recent advances, carbon still is.

4. Steel is also easily repairable: aluminium, carbon and titanium are not. In fact, a small crack in the chain stay on a carbon frame often means the whole frame is destined for the bin. Crucially, steel can be repaired anywhere in the world by a man with a blowtorch and a welding rod. I know this, because I bent a steel bike in northern India, when I was riding around the world. I was slipstreaming a tractor on the Grand Trunk Road near Amritsar. We were going downhill at a lick when I rode into a pothole the size of a hot tub. There was no time to react. I had what American mountain bikers call a 'yard sale'. The bike, panniers, sunglasses, water bottles, tent, pump, map and I were strewn across the tarmac. I lost a lot of skin but the bike took the brunt of it: the top tube and the down tube were both bent, leaving the front wheel shunted backwards, rubbing against the underside of the down tube. I wondered if my round-the-world ride was over.

It took me an afternoon to find the best mechanic, or 'top foreman' as the locals called him, in Amritsar. Expertly, he removed the handlebars, the stem, the forks and the stressed headset from the head tube, while attendants handed him tools as a nurse attends a surgeon. Then he shoved a metal spike through the head tube and literally bashed the tubes straight again. It was terrifying to watch. Thirty minutes later, he'd reassembled the bike. The job cost me 100 rupees (about $2.25) and a packet of smokes. I still had 7,500 miles to go to reach home. The two bent tubes had to be welded again in Gilgit, Tashkent and then Meshad, in Iran, but I did get home, on the same bike. The bare frame, still bearing the wounds, is on the wall in my shed.

For years after my return, I was reluctant to take the frame back to the frame-builder, Roberts Cycles. The marks left by the Iranian welder were heinous. When I eventually did go back, I explained to Chas Roberts what had happened. He was delighted. He thrust me into the retail part of the shop where two men were about to wheel away their brand-new expedition touring bikes – one to cross America, the other to circumnavigate Australia. 'Here,' Chas said, 'listen to Rob's story. This is why you've bought steel frames.'

I have no immediate plans to head off on a trans-continental journey on my dream bike, and, anyway, it's not going to be a touring bike. One day, though, I plan to do some 'credit card touring' on it – that's touring with no luggage except for a wallet. I hope to be off the map on it. I'll be in a town on a former slave-trading route at the foot of a great mountain range having the frame straightened by a bald welder with one eye, as children skip about shrieking, 'Give one pen!' The frame has to be steel.

We know more about steel than any other material used to build bikes. This alloy of iron and small quantities of other chemicals has been a building block of post-industrial civilization. Today, 95 per cent of all bikes are still made from steel. Most of these are made in China and India from 'mild steel', the cheapest, heaviest form of the alloy. If you've ever jumped on a bike in Asia and wondered if someone's tied a baby elephant to the back, you've ridden a mild steel frame. They are very heavy.

Most of the off-the-rack bikes for sale in western countries are made from lighter, low-carbon steel, generically known as 'hi-tensile', or else they're made from aluminium. 'Hi-ten' steel is still relatively inexpensive to produce, is durable, but is stronger than mild steel so less of it is needed to make a bicycle.

At the top of the pile are many high-quality, low-alloy steels.

All quality steel bikes are made from these senior-grade, light and tremendously strong iron alloys. There are several noted marques producing steel bicycle tubing: Columbus, True Temper, Dedacciai, Tange and Ishiwata. If you're British, though, one name resounds: Reynolds.

Alfred Milward Reynolds ran a factory making nails in Birmingham in the late nineteenth century. In his spare time, he obsessed about a problem that was then exercising the whole bike industry: how do you weld together thin, lighter-weight tubes without weakening the joints? Failure after failure led him to devise a tube with 'ends a greater thickness than the body of the tube', as the original 1897 patent for 'butted tubes' stated, but with the same diameter throughout, so saving on weight without compromising strength. It was a breakthrough for the industry. Bicycle manufacturers set about making the next generation of frames that were both strong and very light.

unsurpassed
for strength with lightness

To carry uncomplainingly, touring load or camping gear . . .
To take in its stride rough hillside tracks and rutted lanes . . .
To give your tour the maximum mileage with the minimum effort . . .
Your cycle MUST be built with REYNOLDS 531 BUTTED Frame Tubes, Forks and Stays.

GUARANTEED BUILT WITH **REYNOLDS** BUTTED TUBES FORKS & STAYS

REYNOLDS TUBE CO. LTD.   TYSELEY . BIRMINGHAM 11   ENGLAND

The Reynolds company went on to make motorcycle tubing during World War I, wing spars for Spitfire fighter planes, tubes for bazookas, wheel rims for Rolls Royces and Concorde engine parts, but this archetypal Midlands manufacturing business always returned to steel bicycle tubes. In the alchemy of designing aircraft tubing, Reynolds stumbled on a manganese-molybdenum alloy that made wonderful bikes. In 1935, the company introduced '531' tubing. It was considered revolutionary. Even now, British cyclists of a certain age go misty-eyed and look away towards the horizon just at the mention of '531'.

For forty years, it was the benchmark of excellence in high-end frame materials. In all, twenty-seven Tour de France wins were recorded on Reynolds frames. Luminaries such as Anquetil, Merckx, Hinault, LeMond and Indurain rode bikes made from double-butted Reynolds tubes. The long association between the professional peloton and Reynolds was broken in the 1990s, however, when elite cyclists turned to carbon and titanium. But just when it looked like steel might be abandoned, Reynolds struck back.

In 2006, the company discreetly introduced '953' – a lightweight stainless steel tubing for racing bikes. It has propelled steel alloy back into the premier league of tubing materials. This specially developed, low-carbon steel alloy containing nickel and chromium has superior strength, which means the tube walls can be extremely thin. It is the new benchmark, ultra-high-strength, steel alloy for bicycles. It's also resistant to corrosion. These outstanding properties make maraging steel, the group of iron alloys to which 953 belongs, useful in diverse fields – fencing blades in foil and épée, firing pins in automatic weapons, and in centrifuges for the enrichment of uranium.

A final point about 953 is that the tubes are straight and round, or roundish. Most expensive, mass-manufactured, modern road-racing bikes have oversized aerofoil or oval-shaped, even curved, tubes. These may improve the performance of elite, professional riders. They may not. Either way, the bikes are ugly. Straight, round tubes may now be old school, but they look better.

★

The Reynolds 953 tubeset was sitting in an open box on the corner of a table when I walked into Jason's workshop. It contained top tube, down tube, seat tube, head tube, two chain stays, two seat stays, two drop-outs and a brake bridge. I held one of the main tubes in my hand and caressed it with my thumb and forefinger. Its weight and sheen gave an impression of quality. I put it carefully back in the box. Jason explained why the three main tubes were slightly different diameters and shapes, with reference to their strengths and the stress that varying forces put on the frame.

'It's the combination of tubes we believe is best for your bike,' he said.

Jason was pacing about, tidying and preparing the workbenches. An elegant single-speed, hard-tail mountain bike leant against a wall. The bulbous wings and grille of an MGB sports car peaked from under a dustsheet in one corner. In another, there was a large armoury of tools: hacksaws, drills, files, wire brushes, bottom bracket taps, head tube reamers, a milling machine, pliers, spanners, ratchets and several things I didn't recognize. In the centre of the workshop was the jig, a small piece of scaffolding that holds the tubes in place, to maintain their precise alignment while they are being welded together.

'First, we cut the tubes roughly to length,' Jason said, pulling one from the box and holding it up. 'I've already done this. Now I'm going to mitre the ends of the tubes so they butt up perfectly . . . so there's maximum metal contact at the joint and we get a really good weld.'

Suddenly the room was booming with a raucous, metallic noise. Orange sparks were flying out of one corner. Jason was grinding the steel tube down on a huge belt sander.

'It doesn't half wear the belts through fast,' he said, pausing to check the mitre. 'But it's that strong this 953, you can't use a metal cutter on it. You can't use a lathe or a mill to do this, so we pretty much hand-built this sand-belt mitring machine. We call it "homebrew". In the old days, when we built more traditional frames with lugs, the mitre wasn't quite so important. But with TIG welding, it's got to be immaculate.'

I had thought about a frame made the traditional way, using steel lugs that fit over the ends of the tubes like sockets, and join them together. From the late nineteenth century until the 1970s – most of the history of the bicycle – it was the preferred way to build high-end steel frames, largely because the lugs meant tubes could be thinner and lighter. Advances in metallurgy, as well as the introduction of TIG and MIG welding processes, have effectively negated any advantage. Today, to have a lugged frame is basically a cosmetic decision. It generally costs a bit more, too.

From the 1930s to the 1960s, British frame-builders obsessed about lugs. It was perhaps the vestige of a refined aesthetic that had prevailed among British artisans since the beginning of the Industrial Revolution. A bespoke bicycle workshop would have employed one frame-builder, a painter and the filer, who hand-filed standard steel lugs into ornate objects of art. The sheer beauty of a builder's lugs became the benchmark of his craftsmanship.

Many British builders were known for their outstanding lugged steel frames, but one marque stood out in the attempts to beautify the bicycle – Hetchins. Russian-born Hyman Hetchin fled the Revolution in 1917, aged 26, and began selling bicycles out of his north London home in the 1920s. He sold frames made by local builders, one of whom was Jack Denny. Denny believed longer lugs would make a stronger frame; and longer lugs meant more room for decoration. Denny and Hetchin also patented curly seat and chain stays. The bikes, with model names like *Nulli Secundus* and *Magnum Opus II*, were crowned with rococo 'lugs of distinction'. Today, Hetchins frames are highly sought after

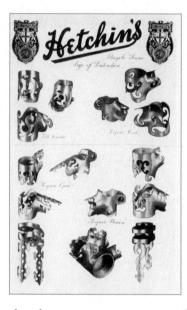

by collectors, though the frou-frou lugwork certainly isn't to everyone's taste.

The obsession with lugs has recently crossed the Atlantic. Several of the revered American artisans making bespoke bicycles today were apprenticed in London and Milan in the 1970s. They took the ailing tradition of lug-cutting back and nursed it. The new wave of young, idealistic US frame-builders has embraced it. In Britain, you only read about lug-cutters in the obituary pages on vintage bicycle collectors' websites.

When the firework display was over, Jason began preparing the jig. He worked quickly but there was an ease even in his hastiest movements. His hands appeared to be pre-programmed. They were often completing one job while his mind was clearly attending to the next. I wondered if this was a mark of his artisanship. It was certainly a reflection of his experience: he builds five frames a week.

When the jig was set up and the tubes clamped in place, he checked everything over, reverting one last time to the piece of paper pinned to the wall with the measurements for my frame. 'Head 73°; Seat 74°,' he said to himself, like an incantation.

Jason was referring to the two angles that are fundamental to the geometry of the frame: the angles of the head tube and the seat tube. The geometry of a frame – that is the angles between the tubes of a frame – is largely determined by the intended application of the bicycle. Criterium, triathlon, time trial, touring and sportive bikes are all variations of the road bike, for different purposes. They may look roughly the same shape, but in fact they each have a different geometry, giving them different ride characteristics. Mountain and commuter bikes have a different geometry again.

Frame geometry is an important factor in how a bicycle rides, how comfortable it is, how it responds to a rider's manoeuvres, how it corners, descends and even climbs. Many other factors also affect ride quality – from the frame and fork materials to tyre

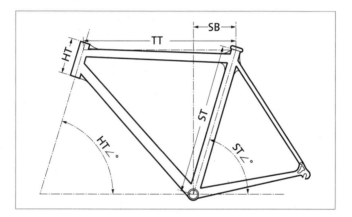

pressure – but the geometry of a frame sets the parameters. Few cyclists ever think about frame geometry. If you buy a mass-manufactured bike, it's scarcely a consideration. When I brought up the subject of frame geometry with a friend, he said: 'Rob, just how long is your beard going to be when you've finished this book?' And he's a cyclist.

Along with the immaculate fit and the right tubing material, geometry is an intrinsic part of buying a bespoke bicycle. Get the geometry of the frame wrong and you could end up with a bike that is at best uncomfortable, and at worst, dangerous to ride. Get it right, and the bike will have the handling characteristics you desire.

Seat tube angle: measured in degrees relative to the horizontal plane (ST∠° in the diagram), they can vary from 65° to 80°. Steeper angles (75°–80°) push the rider's weight forward on to the handlebars and are less comfortable over long distances, but more aerodynamic; they are common on dedicated time-trial bikes, track bikes and triathlon bikes with aero bars. Slack angles (65°), which place more weight on the saddle, belong on commuter or other bikes for short trips. Conventional road-racing bikes with drop handlebars tend to be between 72° and 75°. The angle is partly determined by ergonomics – that is, the saddle being in the best position for efficient pedalling. The seat tube angle on my bike is 74°.

Head tube angle: again, measured in degrees relative to the horizontal plane (HT∠° in the diagram), it has a marked effect on steering characteristics and shock absorption and can vary from 71° to 75°. Steeper angles mean a bike handles more quickly – turn your head and the bike turns too (such bikes are often described as 'twitchy' or 'Italian style' and are favoured by pro racers for criteriums – short road races round city centres, with many tight corners and a densely packed peloton). Slack angles make a bike more stable, notably on descents, and generally more comfortable over long distances. Touring bikes have slack angles. The head tube angle on my bike is 73° – bang in the middle and accepted for at least seventy years as the optimum angle for a road bike. Tour de France style bikes, sometimes known as 'stage racing' bikes, commonly have a head angle of around 73°: it's sporty but sensible.

Other geometric measurements that contribute significantly to the ride characteristics of a bicycle are the wheelbase – the distance between the front and rear hubs – and the height of the bottom bracket. Both, again, affect the handling. Brian determined the geometry of my bike taking account of my physique, my experience and the type of riding I plan to do. The result will be a sportive-style bike: the handling will feel sharp, but the bike will be comfortable enough to sit on all day, and stable when I'm steaming down a mountain in the Dolomites at 45 mph.

Unless you are a very experienced rider, you'll struggle to distinguish between two sportive-style bikes with a one-degree difference in the head-tube angle, but ride a triathlon bike and then jump on a touring bike and you get the message. Be warned though; the more you learn about geometry, the faster your beard will grow.

'We're ready to weld, Rob. You know you can't observe TIG welding with the naked eye. It can burn your eyes out. It's called "flash burn". It's like someone's chucked broken glass in your eyes. Best avoided, so here's a mask.'

The TIG process entails welding tubes directly together, in a blanket of inert gas, using a tungsten welding element. The tungsten acts as a torch, heating up the tubes and the filler metal, which is fed into the weld during the process. Originally developed in the aerospace industry, it was Californian BMX frame-builders who introduced the process to the bicycle in the early 1980s. It was a grassroots innovation that went into the mainstream very quickly.

With the mask on, I felt like Darth Vader in a village pantomime. Jason adjusted the settings on the control panel of the welder and checked the tungsten electrode. There was a great snapping sound, like a wet flag straightening in a gale, and the torch was lit. It could have been the inspiration for a light-sabre, I thought. With huge leather gloves on, and a filler rod in one hand, Jason set the torch to the tubes.

'I'm just tacking it in first,' he said, 'to fix the joint. Then we'll get rid of the clamp and weld it properly.' The jig rotated on a horizontal axis, and Jason worked round the first joint with steady hands. When the head, seat and down tubes were welded with surgical cleanliness, he began work on the top tube: mitring, checking the tube against the frame and mitring again, over and over until he was satisfied. The front triangle was taking shape. Bare, and without stays, it looked fragile.

'It's too easy to blow a hole through 953, the tubing is that thin and delicate. Mistakes are very expensive,' Jason said. 'I have to concentrate so hard, like. That's why I won't have people in the workshop when I'm welding. You're a very rare exception, Rob, and that's only because Dad bent my ear.'

Next Jason used the jig to set the wheelbase length of the frame. 'I'm setting the frame for a 23 mm tyre, as you agreed with Dad. The edge of your tyre will come to here,' he said, placing a finger on the jig, a short distance behind the bottom of the seat tube, 'but the frame will actually take any tyre from 18 to 28 mm in diameter. If you were having mudguards, or what have you, then we'd set it back here a little, but with you having pretty well a race bike, really, it'll be here.'

Jason set to work on the chain stays, cutting them first with a hacksaw, and then shaving them down on old Homebrew. Again, it was trial and error – shave a bit, hold it up to the frame, shave a little more . . . repeat until perfect. I was amazed at how much of the work was done by eye.

'Because no two humans are the same, no two frames are the same,' he said, snapping the stay against the frame and the jig with a soft, metallic 'tch-ik'. 'I'd love to be able to pre-mitre twenty chain stays in a batch and just pop 'em in, but you can't. Every joint has to be handmade. And that's why it'll only fit you right. Why it'll be perfectly balanced, just for you.'

The seat stays were the last tubes to be welded: they would complete the rear triangle, and the diamond shape. There are several ways to affix the top of the seat stays to what is called the 'seat cluster' – the junction of the seat tube and the top tube. As with lugs, the method of attaching seat stays developed among British and Italian frame-builders during the twentieth century, as a way of distinguishing who built the bike – it was like a signature, and a mark of the pride an artisan took in identifying himself with his work. It is the aesthetic flourish underpinned with practical design that typifies the frame-builder's artistry.

The different methods include 'fastback', 'semi-fastback', 'Hellenic' and 'wishbone'. At Rourke's, they favour what is widely recognized as the strongest way to attach the seat stays, whereby they are mitred to wrap right around the seat cluster and rejoin above it.

'The "wrapover" seat stay has been something of a Rourke trademark for the last 30 years,' Jason said when he'd finished mitring. 'I'll be honest: it's a right headache, but it looks great. At least, we think so.'

The torch snapped alight again. We flipped our visors down. Jason picked up a fresh filler rod and the flame roared into action on the seat cluster. He worked methodically round the weld, turning the jig, flicking the cable of the torch from beneath his feet, holding the flame steady at the exact distance from the weld. Ten minutes later, the seat stays were on. The torch went out. Jason pulled off his mask and stepped back, inviting me forward with one arm, like a midwife in a maternity ward introducing an overawed father to his child. The frame of my dream bike – the diamond soul – was finished.

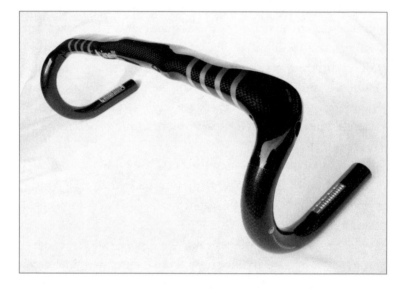

2. Drop Bars, Not Bombs

Steering System

Life is like riding a bicycle. To keep your balance,
you must keep moving.

(Albert Einstein)

In April 1815 the Indonesian volcano Mount Tambora erupted, and continued doing so for three months. An estimated 90,000 people died. It remains the biggest eruption in recorded history. Millions of tons of volcanic ash were blasted into the earth's upper atmosphere, forming an aerosol veil that shut out solar radiation across Europe and North America. The sun disappeared, rainfall increased and average temperatures fell several degrees. It is probably the most dramatic incident of global cooling the world has ever known.

The social ramifications were immense. In New England there were blizzards in July. Many farmers were wiped out, prompting both the rapid settlement of New York and expansion into the mid-west. In Ireland, 65,000 starved to death. In England there were food riots and the dramatic colours of the dust-laden sunsets inspired a young landscape artist, J. M. W. Turner. Byron wrote his poem *Darkness*. In Switzerland, the endless winter moved the 18-year-old Mary Shelley to write *Frankenstein*.

In 1816, known as the 'year without a summer', the harvest

failed across the Western world. The role of the price of oats was then something like the price of oil today. In southern Germany 'true famine' prevailed, according to the historian Carl von Clausewitz. There, farmers who could no longer afford oats to feed their horses, shot them. An eccentric German aristocrat, Baron Karl von Drais de Sauerbronn, a former student of mathematics at Heidelberg University and inventor, witnessed the slaughter. Without horse power, society faced an even graver crisis. Inspired by necessity, Drais realized a dream as old as mankind: he conceived a mechanical horse with wheels.

The 'Draisine' was invented in 1817. It was the first prototype bicycle. Also known as a *'laufmaschine'* ('running-machine'), it comprised two wooden carriage wheels in line, a wooden bench which the rider straddled, and an elementary steering system. You didn't pedal. You propelled it by scooting or paddling your feet along the ground: travelling downhill or at speed, you lifted both feet off the ground.

It was original. No one had previously put a pair of wheels in line, on a frame, and made use of the fundamental precept of the bicycle: balance by steering. It was thought then that without your feet on the ground, you'd fall over. The Draisine taught humanity that you can balance on two wheels in line if, and only if, you can steer.

One of the big, unanswered questions in the history of the bicycle is: why, when technology had made it feasible for at least 3,500 years, did the Draisine take so long to invent? A hypothesis is that no one believed you could actually balance on two in-line wheels. It is possible that Drais only worked it out himself by chance. He may have anticipated stabilizing the machine by almost constant use of the feet: only when it was built, and he was ripping down a hill did he raise his feet from the ground and realize he could achieve the same with the help of the steering mechanism.

By imparting velocity to a machine, Drais also accelerated the act of walking or running, while simultaneously reducing the energy consumption required. To prove his point, he rode from Mannheim, where he lived, to the Schwetzinger Relaishaus and back in an hour, along Baden's best road. The same journey took three hours on foot.

With hindsight, we know that the Draisine was the earliest ancestor of the bicycle. At the time, it did not make a significant impression. The machine was expensive, cumbersome and weighed some 100 lb. The poet John Keats scornfully called it 'the nothing of the day'. It was ahead of its time. Roads, especially in winter, were generally too awful to ride on. By 1820 the machines had been banned from pavements in Milan, London, New York, Philadelphia and Calcutta. In Europe, when the harvests recovered, the Draisine fell into obscurity and the dream of a mechanical horse was abandoned for forty years. Ironically, the Draisine is now having a popular renaissance – in the form of a toy bike thought to be *the* ideal way to help children learn balance. It's a fine example of things going full circle.

Today, we take the ability to ride a bicycle for granted. This is partly because we think it's easy – once learnt, never forgotten – and partly because the vast majority of us learn when we are children. It was not always so. Throughout the history of the bicycle, adults attended 'riding schools' to learn how to maintain the machine in equilibrium, just as we take driving lessons

today. Denis Johnson, an enterprising London coach-maker who custom-made Draisines, opened the first riding school in Soho, in 1819. He charged a shilling a lesson, catering for the upper-class Regency dandies, among whom the machine was fashionable for a summer, hence its nickname, the 'dandy-horse'.

The next great evolutionary leap for the bicycle happened in Paris during the 1860s: rotary cranks and pedals were attached to the front wheel of the Draisine and the 'velocipede' was born. In 1868–70 it sparked a fashionable craze – 'velocipede mania' – on both sides of the Atlantic. The addition of pedals meant the rider's feet were off the ground all the time. Since the pedals were attached to the front wheel, the handlebar had to be braced against the side-to-side effect of pedalling and, when turning, the steering was encumbered by the pressure of pedalling, due to the mis-alignment between the leg and the plane the pedal rotates in. In consequence, everyone went to 'school' to learn how to ride. The first Parisian velocipede manufacturer, Michaux et Compagnie, opened an indoor training school in 1868, beside their new factory. Free lessons were given to people who bought velocipedes; the rest hired instructors by the hour. After half a dozen lessons, riders were sent out to brave the streets.

When a velocipede from Paris was demonstrated at a gymnasium in London in 1869, people were amazed. The magazine *Ixion: A Journal of Velocipeding, Athletics, and Aerostatics*, carried a report by John Mayall, later a great advocate for cycling:

I shall never forget our astonishment at the sight of Mr. Turner whirling himself round the room, sitting on a bar above a pair of wheels in a line that ought, as we innocently supposed, to fall down immediately . . . I turned to Mr. Spencer and exclaimed, 'by Jove, Charley, there's a balance!'

Later the same year, an article in the periodical *Scientific American* breathlessly concluded: 'That a velocipede should maintain an upright position is one of the most surprising feats of practical mechanics.'

In April 1869, the Pearsall brothers opened their 'Grand Velocipede Academy or Gymnaclidium' on Broadway, New York. Hundreds of influential citizens attended to try out the new craze. The famous acrobatic brothers, the Hanlons, also opened a school. Some 'velocinasiums' advertised women-only classes, and hired female instructors. Books of riding instructions were published. Entrepreneurs quickly spread the craze for riding 'academies' or 'rinks' across the country: by late spring, Boston had twenty schools, most major cities had at least a dozen and every small town had one.

In 1869 an American journalist summed up the reasons these schools were so popular:

Velocipedes are pretty things to look upon as they whirl along so swiftly and gracefully, operated by some practiced hand. But did you ever try to ride one? It seems an easy thing to sit on the little carpeted seat, put your feet upon the treadles, and astonish everybody by your speed; but

just try it! And don't invite your lady friends to witness that first performance either. You mount the machine with a great deal of dignity
and confidence, you see that all is clear, you undertake to place your
feet in the proper position, and – the trouble begins. Your first half
hour is spent [deciding] which shall be uppermost, yourself or the
machine, and the machine exhibits an amount of skill and perseverance
that astonishes you.

When the velocipede evolved into the 'high-wheeler' or
'ordinary' in 1870 (the nickname 'penny-farthing' was only used
later), having an instructor was highly advisable. The pedals were
still attached to the front wheel, inhibiting the steering, the rider
was seated high over the front wheel and there was now a long,
long way to fall. Again, a plethora of riding schools sprang up,
usually associated with a bicycle manufacturer. When Columbia
Bicycles relocated its headquarters in Connecticut, the *à la mode*
offices featured, on the fifth floor, 'the most complete riding
school in existence'.

In 1884, at the age of 48, Mark Twain said, 'I confessed to
age by mounting spectacles for the first time, and in the same
hour, I renewed my youth, to outward appearance, by mounting
a bicycle for the first time. The spectacles stayed on.' Twain's
essay, *Taming the Bicycle*, on learning to ride a high-wheeler with
a hired instructor or 'Expert', illustrates well the perils of the
machine:

He [the Expert] said that the dismounting was perhaps the hardest
thing to learn, and so we would leave that to the last. But he was in
error there. He found, to his surprise and joy, that all that he needed
to do was to get me on to the machine and stand out of the way; I could
get off, myself. Although I was wholly inexperienced, I dismounted
in the best time on record. He was on that side, shoving up the machine;

we all came down with a crash, he at the bottom, I next, and the machine on top.

After several further attempts – 'the result as before . . . you don't get down as you would from a horse, you get down as you would from a house afire' – Twain did finally mount the machine:

We got up a handsome speed, and presently traversed a brick, and I went out over the top of the tiller and landed, head down, on the instructor's back, and saw the machine fluttering in the air between me and the sun. It was well it came down on us, for that broke the fall, and it was not injured. Five days later I got out and was carried down to the hospital, and found the Expert doing pretty fairly. In a few more days I was quite sound. I attribute this to my prudence in always dismounting on something soft. Some recommend a feather bed, but I think an Expert is better.

The Expert returned to the fray with four assistants and Twain eventually learnt to balance and steer:

The bicycle had what is called the 'wabbles,' and had them very badly. In order to keep my position, a good many things were required of me, and in every instance the thing required was against nature. That is to say, that whatever the needed thing might be, my nature, habit, and breeding moved me to attempt it in one way, while some immutable and unsuspected law of physics required that it be done in just the other way . . . For instance, if I found myself falling to the right, I put the tiller hard down the other way, by a quite natural impulse, and so violated a law, and kept on going down. The law required the opposite thing – the big wheel must be turned in the direction in which you are falling. It is hard to believe this, when you are told it . . . The intellect has to come to the front, now. It has to teach the limbs to discard their old education and adopt the new.

Twain memorably concludes: 'Get a bicycle. You will not regret it, if you live.'

Many who rode high-wheelers didn't. With the arrival of the safety bicycle in 1885, the world finally had a machine that was both safe (at least compared to the high-wheeler) and easy to steer. Since the pedals were attached via a chain to the rear wheel, the front wheel was free again to undertake its principal responsibility – steering. Only the aged and the overly prudent required 'experts' now. Leo Tolstoy, aged 67, took instruction in 1895 and Jerome K. Jerome reported how, around the same time in London's parks, 'elderly countesses [and] perspiring peers, still at the wobbly stage, battled bravely with the laws of equilibrium; occasionally defeated, they would fling their arms round the necks of hefty young hooligans who were reaping a rich harvest as cycling instructors: "Proficiency guaranteed in twelve lessons."'

For the greater part of humanity, balancing on a safety bicycle was straightforward. In *The Complete Cyclist*, published in 1897, A. C. Pemberton wrote: 'What each learner must remember is simply to turn the handles in the direction in which he is falling ... the rest is easy' – a fact that lies at the heart of the universal appeal of the bicycle to this day.

Bicycling Science, an academic tome on the physics behind the machine, explains balancing a bike as: 'making the small support motions necessary to counter each fall as soon as it starts, by accelerating the base horizontally in the direction in which it is leaning, enough so that the acceleration reaction (the tendency of the centre of mass to get left behind) overcomes the tipping effect of unbalance'.

Perhaps Twain put it better but the point is that balance is at the heart of the story of the bicycle. Drais understood this, even if he did discover it by accident. And the key to balancing a bicycle is learning to steer the handlebars the way the bicycle is leaning, putting the centre of mass back over its support, and regaining equilibrium. Only temporarily, of course, for a bicycle follows more or less a curving trajectory, continually deviating a little to one side or the other. I've often wondered if it is this – the eternal serpentine course of the bicycle, the 'dignified curvature of path' as H. G. Wells called it – that lies at the root of my love for the machine.

Initially a child learning to ride a bike will refuse to steer the way the bike is leaning; once this is grasped, the child will over-correct, yanking the handlebars to left and right, veering dramatically from side to side like a sailor on shore leave full of rum. In time, the steering adjustments become more subtle, and second nature.

If you restrain or lock the steering on a bicycle, you cannot ride it. If you've ever got the front wheel of a bike stuck in a tram track, or off-road in a narrow rut, you'll know what I mean. In addition, a bicycle has to be moving forward to balance. Balancing a bicycle at rest – a manoeuvre known as a 'track stand' – is difficult. The fixed-wheel riders you see at city traffic lights managing to balance their bikes without dabbing a foot down are only nominally at rest. With the front wheel set at an angle, they are minutely rolling the bicycle backwards and forwards. They are also showing off. I know. I used to do it.

For a year I became obsessed with not putting a foot down whenever I cycled in London. Being able to do a track stand at traffic lights was one of the skills required: anticipating lights and braking early, knowing when to run them on amber and intuiting the manoeuvres of motorists were also critical. I regularly used

to get from my flat in Paddington, north of Hyde Park, to the
college in the City where I studied photo-journalism, without
ever dabbing a foot down. That was easy: 4 miles – I knew the
sequence of the lights at the major intersections and my route
avoided main roads. More difficult was riding from Paddington
to Camberwell, south of the River Thames, where my girlfriend
lived. If I arrived and rode up the garden path, grinning like a
fool, she knew I'd done it. 'You make people who won't walk on
the cracks in the pavement look normal. You should seek help,'
she'd say. The relationship didn't last.

Even today, there is a small minority of adults who can't ride
a bicycle, let alone pull a track stand: roughly 8 per cent of women
and 1 per cent of men in Britain, according to a recent Transport
for London survey. Apparently, most able-bodied adults can grasp
the rudiments in one three-hour session. The best thing about
learning to ride a bicycle, though, is that you will only have to
do it once.

There is a neuroscientific explanation for why we never forget
how to ride a bicycle. We have a type of nerve cell in our brain
that controls the formation of memories for motor skills. They're
called 'molecular layer interneurons'. These nerve cells encode
electrical signals leaving the cerebellum – the part of the brain
that controls co-ordinated movement – into a language that can
be stored as memory in other parts of the brain. Of course, our
molecular layer interneurons don't only encode the skills required
to ride a bicycle; they encode all motor skills, from crawling to
skiing and from knitting to dancing the tango.

What this doesn't explain is why riding a bicycle has been
singled out as the one shared experience that we reference to
illustrate how something once learnt can be etched in the memory
so distinctly that we take it to the grave. 'It's like riding a bike'
– we say this about something we never forget how to do. Why

not the expression 'like rowing a boat', 'like using chopsticks' or 'like doing breast stroke' instead? For some reason, we've chosen riding a bike as the benchmark motor skill by which our molecular layer interneurons may be judged. I don't know why. I'm not sure if anyone does.

It may be to do with the relationship between the bicycle and childhood. As I've said, most of us now learn to ride a bike early in life, 'before the dark hour of reason grows', as John Betjeman put it. Perhaps, in youth, the cerebellum sends out stronger electrical signals, which are in turn encoded very carefully and stored in a secure place – the cerebral equivalent of a safe-deposit box in a steel vault beneath a bank in Zurich. Or perhaps it's to do with the fact that riding a bicycle fits so perfectly with the human software that our molecular layer interneurons can encode the motor skills and guarantee that the files won't be corrupted for the life of the user.

It may also be to do with how incredibly well balanced the safety bicycle is. It's so well balanced, it doesn't need a rider at all. If you let a well-aligned, riderless bicycle, with freely turning steering, roll down an incline, it will remain straight and upright, up to a speed which depends on its design. A riderless bicycle can even automatically make the small steering motions necessary to right itself after a bump or disturbance of some kind. Physicists call this 'intrinsic stability'. It is often written that the gyroscopic momentum of a bicycle's spinning wheels alone support a riderless bike, like a spinning top. This is not true. The gyroscopic effect is one of several subtle concepts, including geometry and the distribution of mass, behind a self-balancing vehicle.

With or without a rider, a bicycle does need a well-balanced and maintained steering system to remain upright. This comprises the handlebars, the handlebar stem, the front forks and the headset. The forks have a steering tube, which passes through the head tube of the frame; the stem and handlebars are clamped to the steering tube. The headset is principally made up of two bearing assemblies or cups that are pressed into the top and the bottom of the head tube of the frame. The headset permits the forks to rotate independently of the frame, for steering and balance.

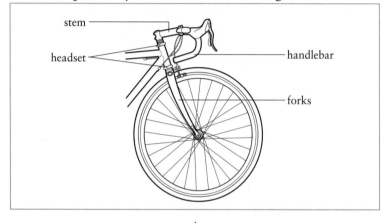

★

'We think of it as an initiative test,' Chris DiStefano said, greeting me with a big handclap at the door of an unmarked, unassuming factory down the end of Nela Street, a dead-end road that had neither a sign nor any road markings, at the arse-end of a large industrial estate in north-west Portland, Oregon. Finding Chris King Precision Components had taken half a morning. I'd asked directions two dozen times: 'Nope. 'Fraid I ain't never heard of that place,' came the reply every time. It seemed strange. The company has a reputation for making superbly engineered bicycle components – hubs, bottom brackets and, most notably, headsets. That reputation has reached around the planet and yet people who worked a block away had never heard of Chris King. Hell, they'd never even heard of Nela Street. It was confirmation of something I learnt a long time ago travelling on a bicycle: if you want local knowledge, don't, for

God's sake, ask a local. In the end, I'd found it, as one first finds
equilibrium on a bicycle, by trial and error.

Chris DiStefano is the marketing director at Chris King. When
I'd first emailed him with an outline of my project, and the idea
that I might visit the factory to see the headset for my dream bike
being made, the shutters were snapped shut: no comprehensive
tours, no photography of the facility allowed, no 'walk-up orders'
for components. An interview with Chris King himself was,
Chris DiStefano wrote, 'not an option. Bummer, I know, I'm
nothing but bad news.' Thankfully, by my arrival, Chris had
warmed up, though meeting Chris King was definitely not going
to happen: he was 'on holiday'.

'Everybody else's tour ends here,' Chris said, standing in the
door between the reception and the factory. He was lithe, like a
committed amateur cyclist, with the long arms of a boxer and
the unpredictable gesticulations of a stand-up comedian. 'But
because it's your *dream* bicycle, *and* you've come all the way from
Wales, we've decided to invite you beyond the red door.'

We walked through the finishing and component assembly
area: headsets were being stacked and packaged – 'every one
destined for somebody's dream bike,' Chris said – and in one
corner, a laser machine was engraving hubs with the company
logo. Chris explained how the people who work in each area
design the workspace. There are fewer than 100 employees, but
it helps them claim a sense of ownership of the company.

'Chris King got into this business in 1976. He was a keen
touring cyclist and he'd heard too many complaints about faulty
headsets from his cycling friends,' Chris said. 'With his engineering experience making medical equipment, he thought he could
do better, and he designed the first *sealed* bearing headset.'

We'd reached a metal balcony overlooking the 'prototype and
development' area of the machine shop. Only one machine was

working and I wondered if work on prototypes had been shut down for my visit. If you were involved in headset espionage, and in the trade of bicycle engineering secrets generally, writing a book about assembling your dream bicycle would be a good cover.

The headset is an unglamorous but fundamental component of the bicycle. It's also a part that takes a terrific beating from the road. The ball bearings contained within the lower cup of a headset are loaded differently from those in all other rotating parts of the bicycle. They are loaded axially, and they hardly rotate – an undesirable situation as impacts from the road are transferred to stationary ball bearings. This is called 'thrust stress' and it can cause pitting or brinelling of the bearings. The problem is exacerbated riding off-road, or on a loaded touring bicycle.

'With the advent of the mountain bike, the problem of poor steering components was amplified,' Chris said. We were walking through the main machine shop: it was alive with the buzz and thrust, the boom, drone and rattle of metal being engineered into life. 'You ride a mountain bike, right? The headset gets jack-hammered. And if you ride in a place where the weather is wet, life is even tougher for a headset. So you need good bearings. And that's what we do here – we make great bearings. Yes, we do make beautiful aluminium pieces in an array of lovely colours to house those bearings, and people justifiably call our components "bike jewellery". But really, what we do is make great ball bearings.'

The bicycle industry was the first to make widespread use of ball bearings, though the concept was understood much earlier. Galileo described them around 1600. Leonardo da Vinci wrote about them a century before that, and remains of wooden ball bearings have been found on Roman galleys and dated to around

40 AD. How bearings work is very simple: if two surfaces roll over each other, rather than slide, friction is greatly reduced. On a modern bicycle, there are bearings – spherical hard steel balls embedded in lubricant – between the fixed and rotating parts of the hubs, the bottom bracket, the pedals, the freewheel and the headset. Without bearings, riding a bicycle would be like pedalling a sleigh.

On a cold, wet day in Paris in November 1869, the humble ball bearing made a dramatic entry into the history of the bicycle. Over 100 cyclists, including a handful of women, were gathered beneath the Arc de Triomphe in Paris, before a crowd of thousands. At 7.30 a.m, a flag was waved and the riders set off for the city of Rouen, 75 miles to the north-west.

This was the world's first organized bicycle road race. On desperately poor roads, it was the most ambitious test of man and the machine yet. The prize was 1,000 francs. The victor was James Moore, an Englishman who had grown up in Paris, across the street from a family of blacksmiths called Michaux who were makers of velocipedes. Moore, known as the 'Flying Frenchie' in Britain and the 'Anglais Volant' in France, went on to become one of the best known cyclists of his day. He won many races, set the record for the distance cycled in an hour and held several world championship titles, but he is best remembered for winning the first Paris–Rouen race.

The staging of the Paris–Rouen race was disrupted in 1870

by the outbreak of war between France and Prussia, but it was used as the model for all the classic European road races that were to follow, and which endure today. Each new race – Bordeaux–Paris, a 350 mile night–day event inaugurated in 1891, Paris–Brest–Paris also in 1891, Liège–Bastogne–Liège in 1892, Paris–Roubaix in 1896 and the Tour de France in 1903, to name a few – all seemed to try and outdo their predecessors. But Paris–Rouen set the first marker in the lasting relationship between bicycle racing and human suffering. Moore is reputed to have said before the race, 'I will get there first, or they will find my body in the road.'

It is a heroic sentiment – a sentiment that has been a corner-stone of road cycle racing ever since; a sentiment that has provided an endless resource for the marketing of road racing bicycles, componentry, clothing, holidays, newspapers, books, films and the races themselves. Of course, it's also the sentiment that has blindly condoned drug abuse within the sport for a century, and the sentiment that killed Tommy Simpson in the 1967 Tour de France: they really did find his body in the road, with amphet-amines and cognac in his blood, 1 mile from the top of the infamous Mont Ventoux. He'd ridden himself to death. He didn't actually say, 'Put me back on the bike', but the epitaph on Simpson's gravestone in the churchyard at Harworth, Notting-hamshire, reads: 'His body ached, his legs were tired but still he would not give in.'

As it happens, Moore's victory in the 1869 Paris–Rouen race was more about technical advantage than human resolve. He was riding the only bike that had ball bearings fitted in the pedal axle. I realize ball bearings aren't as glamorous as the physical and moral fortitude of mankind, but that's the truth. All kinds of machines set off down Avénue de la Grande Armée on 7 November 1869: monocycles, tricycles and quadricycles were among them. James

Moore, and all the other serious racers, rode velocipedes. The race was promoted by the magazine *Le Vélocipède Illustré*, and by the Olivier brothers, owners of Michaux et Compagnie, the successful velocipede manufacturing business.

The exact details of Moore's steed are not established by contemporary reports, sadly. He may have ridden a heavy wooden machine with solid rubber tyres, made by his old family friend, Michaux. Or he may have been on a bicycle specially manufactured for the event by the French mechanic, Suriray. All accounts, however, do agree on one thing: his bicycle that day was the first machine with ball bearings in the pedal axle, ensuring the cranks rotated more smoothly, making pedalling more efficient. Moore won the race by fifteen minutes.

The first patent for ball bearings was granted to Welsh inventor and ironmaster Philip Vaughn in 1794. He used radial ball bearings in carriage axles, to make them easier to pull. Curiously, his idea didn't catch on. Suriray had received the first French patent for ball bearings early in 1869. According to the historian H. O. Duncan, he got convicts at the prison of St Pelagy, near Paris, to grind out by hand the ball bearings for Moore's bike. The problem was that these handmade ball bearings weren't hard-wearing. In fact, early ball bearings wore away to dust quickly enough under the loads applied to them on the bicycle.

In the late 1870s two Birmingham toolmakers, William Bown and Joseph Hughes, registered patents for lubricating bearings and for a ball-bearing race – the smooth ring that the balls sit in – and applied their ideas to bicycle and carriage wheels and roller skates, under the *Aeolus* trademark. Hughes's adjustable ball-bearing race quickly became standard throughout the cycle industry. The big breakthrough came from Germany, though. Friedrich Fischer is considered by bearing enthusiasts everywhere to be the 'Father of the modern ball bearing'. It's not perhaps a distinction many covet, but if you ride bicycles, you have much to thank Fischer for. He invented the ball grinder in 1883; for the first time a machine ground balls to a perfectly round shape, in large volumes. The company he founded is still going strong. It was this, the development of precision steel spheres with extremely hard surfaces, that meant that the ball bearing spread to every rotating part of the bicycle, and subsequently motorbikes, airplanes, automobiles, ships, skateboards, printing presses – pretty much any machine you can think of.

Today, bearings are manufactured using highly sophisticated machinery. How well they work depends on various subtle factors, the most important of which is the quality grade to which they are engineered. Well-manufactured bearings, finished to a high degree of precision, properly configured and assembled, and kept clean and lubricated, can last many millions of revolutions – or a lot of bicycle miles. Yet there is a tendency in bicycle component manufacturing to use bearings made of lighter or cheaper materials, reducing the life of the bearings to a tolerable minimum. I've worn out bearings in hubs, bottom brackets and pedals and I've had headsets fail on me. The latter, however, tend not to fail dramatically – you get a warning that things are going awry. Nonetheless, as soon as the bearings do begin to go, so does the steering. And when you've felt the slightest inaccuracy in the steering, when your unconscious has sent the instructions down to your gloved hands, and the handlebars have gone one way and the front wheel has gone another, you can never trust that bike again.

The number of headsets Chris King produced for the first fifteen years was small, but they attracted a cult following. I'd never seen them advertised, nor even heard anyone speak of them in the UK until about five years ago, when I started to notice them on beautiful bicycles: not necessarily expensive bicycles, but on ones that exuded care and a touch of class.

'Most of our customers are cycling enthusiasts. They appreciate the precision, durability and quality of our components. And they share our philosophy – make something once and make it last,' Chris DiStefano said. We were walking through the main machine shop. It was weirdly clean. Chris pointed out the venting system that extracts the oil 'mist' in the atmosphere and recycles it.

'We don't have model levels,' he continued. 'You don't buy the entry-level CK component and aspire to owning the next grade, then save your money, buy it, replace the old one and work your way up. You just buy one headset. It might live in six different frames. It might live in just one bicycle, for years, a decade, two. The point is to make it once, and make it the best you can make it, so you don't have to extract the materials again.'

It's a good philosophy. It's far from the most profitable approach to manufacturing, but if Chris King is anything to go by, it is one that can work.

'We don't do planned obsolescence. We don't have model years. We don't change products annually. In fact, the 1-inch threaded headset we still sell today is exactly the same as the model Chris King first started making and selling to his friends in 1976.'

We had worked our way back through the rows of now sleeping machines, past the admin offices, where I was shown Chris King's very empty office – 'he's on holiday,' Chris said again, twice – to the door of the canteen. The employees were sitting down to lunch. They looked more like a chapter of Hell's Angels than a light engineering workforce.

'Ah, yes,' Chris said. 'The Portland look. The longer you live here, the more tattoos you have. It works a bit like oak tree rings. Are you hungry? We do good food.'

The menu made for unlikely reading in a company canteen:

eggs Benedict for breakfast, Caesar salad for lunch. 'Food is an important part of Chris King, the person and the company,' the chef, Robert, told me, chopping a chicken breast. Food is an important part of cycling, I thought. Whenever I've been on a bike all day, my appetite is greatest in every sense – greatest in the volume of food I can eat, greatest in the sheer sensory pleasure of eating it, greatest in the atavistic sensation of feeling well fed afterwards. Cycling promotes an appetite that is almost as powerful as lust. Along with the peace and spiritual repletion I feel going to sleep after a long ride, satiating hunger is one of the greatest pleasures in cycling.

'Exactly,' Chris said when I mentioned this. 'Last night, when I got home from a six-hour mountain bike ride – you know, one of those three-hour rides that knows no end – I ate dinner, twice.'

We sat down for lunch with Diane Chalmers, vice-president of operations at Chris King. She explained that the quality of the food in the canteen was part of the initiative to encourage employees to cycle to work:

Mostly it's the obvious stuff – secure bike parking, showers, ventilated lockers – Portland can be very wet – and route advice. We do all of that. One of the more innovative ways to promote cycling is through food. If you ride to work, you get credit, which you can spend in the canteen. The other way is we run two month-long, cycle-commute challenges. If you ride to work every day in either May or September, you earn two extra days of paid holiday, so a maximum of four a year if you do it both months. We're the only people we know who do this. It works well. It generates a greater sense of community within the employees, and it involves us within the wider community, as one of the month challenges is a Portland-wide scheme. But really, we do it just to promote cycling.

I had been drawn to Chris King by the elegance and reliability of their components. I'd half expected to visit a filthy machine shop full of menacing noise and monosyllabic men sucking black coffee through the gaps in their teeth – a crude workplace that James Moore might have recognized. I'd imagined standing in front of a big man in blue coveralls with a ZZ Top beard; me saying 'Are you Chris King?' and him saying, 'So who wants to know?' Instead, I was sitting beside a prepossessing woman in a modern café eating Caesar salad, discussing enlightened pro-cycling policies.

I liked the company, Chris King. In fact, I liked Portland. The city began seriously expanding the bicycle infrastructure in 1993: in the last decade, the number of cyclists has increased tenfold. The people of Portland today make more transport journeys by bicycle per capita than in any other large American city. There is an extensive network of bike lanes, traffic-free paths and bike 'boulevards', as well as signs and pavement markings for cyclists. In the downtown area, the traffic lights are set to control traffic speeds low enough for cyclists to keep up with the flow. You can take a bike on all buses, street-cars and the light rail network. Car-parking spaces have been capped and there are bike racks everywhere. There is an institute at Portland State University devoted to bicycle and pedestrian research. I'd read that people even move house by bicycle: put the word out and a fleet of cyclists will turn up to shift the kitchen sink.

Oregon is home of the timber industry. Fifteen years ago, I cycled across the state. The battle between environmentalists and loggers was in full swing at the time. One day, I was riding down the Pacific Coast Highway, heading to California. From sea level the road rises and falls over a series of steep bluffs. It was raining hard. On one of the descents, wind was buffeting the bike and the spray off the road was blinding. I was tearing downhill when a pick-up truck came past me and braked. When I caught it up on the inside, the truck came menacingly close: a flick of the driver's wrist and I was dead. The passenger window wound down. Through the curtain of water, I could see the brim of a baseball hat, a beard and then teeth. When our eyes met, the man bellowed: 'Ya fuckin' bunny hugger!'

It's quite a turn-around for Portland, the most populous city in Oregon, a city covered in a lattice of eight-lane freeways with no cycling heritage, whose traditional industries are canning and freezing, to become the pedalling capital of America.

'If you make it safe, people will ride,' the Mayor, Sam Adams, told me. We'd met the day before my visit to Chris King, during an annual Portland event called the 'Bridge Pedal': many of the city's streets and the main bridges over the Willamette River were closed for the day, and 17,000 people had taken to two wheels.

'Much of what we've done would be easy for any other city to copy,' Sam said. 'And really, we've just started. Our goal is 25 per cent of all trips in the city to be taken by bike. That's a do-able goal.' An initiative at municipal level has attracted bicycle businesses and bike-minded people from all over the USA to Portland. Chris King relocated here from California.

'You could say Portland has taken ownership of the energy around the bicycle,' Slate Olson told me. Slate moved here from San Francisco and runs the US office of British cycle clothing manufacturer Rapha. We met for coffee on Mississippi Avenue, a bohemian street in north Portland that teems with bicycles all day.

Yes, tens of thousands commute to work by bicycle every day, but also every weekend, 1,200 people ride in cyclo-cross races; there's a gang who make and ride mutant bikes; there's bike polo and bike jousting; every week a bunch of guys go 'zoo-bombing' – that's racing kids' bikes down the hill from Washington Park. We're saturated with cycling sub-cultures. Oh, and we have the largest naked bike ride in America. They say there's a bike event in Portland every twenty-seven minutes. As a politician, you can't get elected without a bike platform. There are at least twenty-five custom frame-builders in business, making Portland the centre of the renaissance in hand-built bicycles. And it's aspirational. A lot of American cities are looking at Portland's cycling scene and wondering: how can we achieve that?

I visited the workshop of Sacha White, a renowned Portland frame-builder. He talked about the re-establishment of small communities within Portland, based around the bicycle:

Fifty per cent of the kids at my children's school cycle there each day. If you live and work and shop locally, then you have a strong community. The big house in the suburbs with a fence around it, then driving ten miles to school and twenty miles to work every day – this destroys communities. I think there's a whole generation re-evaluating that notion of the American dream. Cycling is becoming socially acceptable again. We're trying to assist that by building good bicycles for transportation, bicycles that are truly useful and not just toys.

He was a softly spoken man with a strong vision of what he was doing, and why. He was making bicycles for a brave new world. Needless to say, all his bicycles were fitted with Chris King headsets.

After lunch, Chris DiStefano led me back downstairs to the component assembly area. Sitting on the corner of a workbench was my headset. He clasped my shoulder with one hand and between the forefinger and thumb of the other, he held up the headset above us, to the light: '$1\frac{1}{8}$ "NoThreadSet" with *sotto voce* logo in silver. I guarantee it'll go with whatever colour you paint the bike,' he said. 'It comes with a ten-year warranty – that's how good we think our bearings are. It's a dream headset, for a dream bike.'

The name Cino Cinelli (pronounced 'Chino Chinelli') resonates through the history of modern racing bicycles. Today, you need a degree in chemistry and a Ph.D. in polymeric composite systems to work on R&D in the bicycle industry. Cino Cinelli quit school at 14, in 1930, and acquired an education on the road, racing bicycles. In a professional career that lasted over a decade, he won the Giro di Lombardia, Giro di Piemonte and Giro di Campania. His crowning achievement in the saddle was victory in the gruelling 185 mile, one-day classic race, Milan–San Remo, in 1943.

Convinced that the bicycle was ripe for innovation, Cinelli moved to Milan and set up in business with his brother in 1948. One arm of the company marketed the high-end components of other manufacturers, making Cino a sort of godfather of the industry in Italy: such was the quality of their inventory that simply being included became a mark of distinction. The other arm, developing and selling Cinelli's own innovative products, brought an eminence to the brand that remains today.

With little regard for fashion, Cinelli invested his unconventional ideas in bespoke frame production, making everything from Olympic medal-winning track frames to the 'Supercorsa' road model – an enduring icon of the late twentieth century and the E-type Jaguar of bike frames. In partnership with Unicanitor, Cinelli designed the first plastic-bodied saddle. He invented the first integral sloping fork crown in the 1950s and the M–71, the

first clipless pedal, in the 1970s; he
founded the Italian Association of
Professional Cyclists and wrote
a canonical text on training. Cino
Cinelli and the company he fronted
for three decades are, however, most
famous for handlebars and stems.

Unlike the frame of the bicycle, the
geometry of which varies only a little
according to its intended use, handlebars come in wildly different and
multifarious shapes according to the
type of bicycle they are attached to.
Mountain bikes have flat or 'riser' bars which, as the name suggests,
rise from the centre to the tips. BMX handlebars are U-shaped
and reinforced. Most hybrid or utility bikes have either a straight
bar or a handlebar that curves back towards the rider, ending with
grips parallel to the bike. Similarly, some touring bikes have
these swept-back handlebars, known as 'North Road' bars. The
handlebars on track bikes are characterized by ramps that sweep
down from the centre, straight into the drops or 'D's: they're
designed for use without brake levers and provide more arm
clearance for sprinting out of the saddle. This type of bar has
surged in popularity recently on urban fixed-wheel or single-speed
bikes. Triathlon bikes have 'aero bars', which bring the riders' arms
together and thrust them forward over the front wheel, reducing
the steering capability but increasing aerodynamic efficiency.

The most recognized type of handlebar, though, the bar most
of us would draw on a doodle of a bicycle, is the conventional
drop bar, which you find on all road racing bikes. The significant
advantages of this type of bar lie in the way it promotes even
distribution of weight across the bike, and in the variety of places

you can comfortably put your hands. If you've ever ridden 100 miles in a day, you'll know how prized this variety is. You can sit up with your hands on the flat 'tops' and admire the view; you can rest your hands on the 'ramps' and slipstream the rider in front; hook your hands around the ends and wrench up the steepest inclines out of the saddle; or shove your fists into the Ds and sprint for the line or hare down a mountainside.

When Cino joined his brother Giotto's business in 1948, handlebars were made of steel and fashioned on jigs, by hand. Road racing handlebars were generally a standard shape. From the centre, the bar went straight out then bent forward in a gradual curve; when the bars were parallel with the frame, they turned downwards, bending in a smooth-radius curve through approximately 160°, and straightened at the end. It's a classic and elegant shape.

In the 1950s, Cinelli began to offer subtle differences in the drop, curve-radius, ramp-length and the degree of bend. Models were named after great races, famous climbs and the legends of the age. In the 1950s, Cinelli marketed bar models called 'San Remo', 'Gran Fondo' and 'Giro d'Italia'. In the 1960s, another Italian component manufacturer called TTT, set up by a former engineer at the Ambrosio factory, manufactured 'Bobet', 'Anquetil', 'DeFilippis' and 'Coppi' bars. Drops varied from 145 mm to 210 mm; the length of the ramps, a vertical measurement from the top of the bar to the apex of the bend, ranged from 90 mm to 125 mm.

Giuseppe and Giovani Ambrosio, from Turin, pioneered the use of aluminium in bicycles. They were the first, and for a while only, Italian firm making aluminium bars and stems. More flexible than steel, aluminium was thought to dampen the vibrations from the road. The first aluminium bike was made as early as 1935, but the perception, especially among professional racers, was that this metal wasn't strong enough for handlebars. Today, a similar perception of carbon composites lingers in the peloton: even though the use of carbon fibre in bicycle components has exploded in recent years, some pro riders still insist on having an aluminium bar on their race bike.

Catastrophic handlebar failure, caused by anything from metal fatigue in aluminium to an unnoticed crack in carbon fibre, is something that keeps racers awake at night. If you're going slowly when a handlebar shears without warning, you impale yourself on the stem; if you're tanking down a mountainside in the Alps at 50 mph, you die. Imagine being thrown from a car at the equivalent speed and you get the idea.

When Cinelli switched to manufacturing aluminium handlebars in 1963, opinion among the racing elite changed. Steel handlebars quickly became obsolete, while Cinelli bars became ubiquitous. The model 1 A handlebar stem was introduced in 1964: it became the industry standard. Not only was it inventive in design and strong, it looked fabulous too. For a decade, you rarely saw a professional road cyclist wrap his sinewy fingers round anything else. The company sold 7,500 bars and stems annually in the mid-1960s. By the time Cino retired in 1978, it was 150,000 a year. Despite the growth in production, the standards remained high; the bar and stems were about as coveted as any bicycle components then made. The list of exalted champions – LeMond, Fignon, Hinault, Chiapucci, Cipollini and Armstrong – who have chosen Cinelli bars continues into the present day.

Antonio Colombo, scion of the famous Columbus tubing dynasty, bought Cinelli in 1978. He has continued to drive both companies through design and innovation. Just looking at the contemporary Cinelli catalogue on the company website, I sensed Antonio was eccentric. The impression was confirmed when I

walked into his factory on the outskirts of Milan. He came glid-
ing down the aisle towards me on a scooter, wearing a Paul Smith
suit and hiking shoes.

'Yes, yes, the scooter,' he said after we'd exchanged our 'ciaos',
'the scooter is the best. It has CNC (Computer Numerical
Control) machined components. But it costs more than a bicycle.
Of course, nobody bought it. Except me . . . hah! Shall we have
a tour?'

Antonio's father, Angelo Luigi, established Columbus in 1919
with these words: 'I want to do business in iron and steel and
make a fair and honest profit.' Along with Reynolds, Columbus
dominated the high-end steel bicycle frame market for most of
the twentieth century. At times, they diversified into motorcycles,
ski sticks, car chassis and even tubular steel furniture, but the
racing bicycle was always at the heart of the business. Perhaps the
most significant Columbus innovation was Nivachrome steel
tubing. It was the first alloy developed specifically for building
bicycle frames. Because it loses so little of its strength when
welded, the tubes were thinner and lighter than anything that
had gone before. The bicycle I rode around the world was made
from Nivachrome steel. I told Antonio this when we halted beside
a row of machines where steel tubes were being drawn. He flashed
me a wild look.

I tell you straight, one of the problems for me as a worker, and I started
working in my father's factory when I was 22, was noise – steel tubes
being drawn, steel tubes being cut and moved and banged together . . .
when we made two million tubes a year, when there were 150 frame-
builders in Italy, noise, noise, noise, all day. And then five years ago,
my problem was silence. Everybody wanted carbon. Today, steel is
coming back a little, slowly, particularly in the US. I'm happy to say,
even some Italian frame-builders start to make again in steel. A steel

frame, it lasts for life. OK, carbon is there for competition, but if you want a frame every day for your life, steel . . . we used to make 20,000 tubes at a time. Now we make 20. But we do make again, and look, our workers are happy.

Antonio shouted across a workbench to Emilvano who was bending a cromoly seat stay by hand in a jig. He raised a gloved hand.

'You cannot build a good bicycle with unhappy workers.'

Angelo Luigi Colombo is famous for pioneering steel fork blades with an elliptical (rather than oval) section: these 'Italian section' forks improved the handling characteristics of the bicycle, while making the ride more comfortable. They were enormously popular. Today, Columbus have capitalized on over half a century of experience in fork innovation to produce a range of superb carbon forks – one of the items on my shopping list in Milan.

Antonio led me across the factory to an area where steel tubes, a handlebar and some carbon forks were being tested. Fatigue, shock, static, frontal and side strength – every type of test seemed to be going on, creating an unearthly cacophony: tchik-a-tchik-a-tchik-a . . . dug-dug-dug . . . dink-puhh-dink-puhh. I knew the forks were made in Taiwan. I'd have to make do with watching them being tested for fatigue.

On Brian Rourke's recommendation, I was after a Columbus 'Carve' model. This fork is made with monocoque technology – a construction technique that uses the external skin of a structure, rather than an internal frame, to support loads. Its use in the production of carbon fibre bicycle frames was pioneered in the 1980s and is now widespread. The steering column tube, which is inserted through the head tube, and the fork blades are one piece, made from overlaid layers of carbon. The Carve model has a traditional shape ('Aw, it looks magic,' Brian had said), aluminium forged drop-outs and a rake of 45 mm.

How a bike steers and handles is largely determined by something called 'trail'. If you draw an imaginary line – known as the 'steering axis' – down through the centre of a bicycle head tube, it meets the ground in front of the point where the wheel makes contact with the ground: the horizontal distance between these two points is called the trail (so named because the wheel 'trails' behind the steering axis). A large or long trail makes a bike stable, but relatively slow to turn. A short trail decreases inherent stability but increases agility. The same principles apply to motorbikes. Bicycles made specifically for racing in 'criteriums' – road races around city centres – have a short trail, to aid manoeuvrability. Comfort is not a factor.

Fork rake, sometimes known as 'offset', is the perpendicular distance between the steering axis and the centre of the wheel – so it's a measurement of the forward bend in a fork blade. Along with the angle of the head tube and the radius of the wheel, it is a variable that determines trail. With a given head tube angle

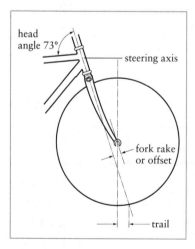

and wheel radius, more fork rake gives less trail and vice versa. Fork rake also affects comfort: touring bikes commonly have a longer fork rake as, combined with a longer wheelbase – the distance between the wheel hubs – it dampens road shock.

Fork rake and the angle of the head tube serve one other design function on a bicycle – to ensure the front wheel clears the feet at the front of the pedal swing. In the early days of the safety bicycle there was very little angling of the head tube and forks. And though history sadly doesn't credit the man who first thought of tilting a bicycle's steering axis, it is more likely to be because of feet striking the wheel than an understanding of stability.

Like hemlines, fork rake has gone up and down in the last century. From the 1930s to the 1950s, bicycles typically had as much as 90 mm of fork rake (and often zero trail): largely because roads were so poor, cyclists demanded bikes with plenty of fork rake and a long wheelbase to absorb the shocks. As roads improved, bikes were built with shorter wheelbases and tyres became narrower, making it necessary to increase trail to ensure the bikes handled safely. Today forks have less rake – 45 mm is average – and generally, the bicycles handle better.

Antonio has rigorously kept innovation within Columbus and Cinelli alive. The bicycle is an 'infinite project', he has written. In fact, he personifies the spirit of ingenuity that, in the middle of the twentieth century, placed Italy instead of Britain at the forefront of the bicycle industry. Cinelli, Campagnolo, Bianchi, Pinarello, De Rosa, Columbus, Selle Italia, TTT, Ambrosio, Colnago, Magistroni, Wilier Triestina – these are the marques that, driven by people's passion for the machine as well as by the commercial boom after World War II, helped the bicycle evolve from a utilitarian machine into an aesthetic object of desire.

The cycle industry in Italy focused obsessively on sport and speed. During the late 1940s, the nation was enthralled by the great rivalry between two Italian giants of cycle racing, Gino Bartali and Fausto Coppi. In 1948, road cycling even spilled over into politics; when the shooting of a prominent Communist politician threatened to cause civil unrest, the Italian Prime Minister rang Bartali during the Tour de France and begged

him to win. It was thought a Bartali victory might divert the
minds of his countrymen from revolution. He duly won and the
threat of unrest passed.

In the 1950s, cycling in Britain was still pervaded by pragmatism
and pastoralism. The road racing scene was hugely undeveloped,
compared with that on the Continent, which helps explain why
so few British cyclists have made a good showing in the Tour de
France. The bicycle was for getting to work during the week,
and for going youth hostelling with a flask of dandelion and
burdock at the weekend. The sport of bicycle racing was still
strangled by the conventions of Victorian rule-makers. It largely
consisted of 'time trials', codified in the 1890s by Frederick
Thomas Bidlake, a man with a passion for time-keeping: competi-
tors set off at intervals and ride alone, against the clock, up and
down a wind-slapped A-road. It's duller than lawn bowling. In
Europe, massed-start rides were much more popular. Races
entailed breakaways and sprint finishes, chases and crashes,
suffering and solidarity, tactics and alliances, co-operation and
competition, vanity and honour. Massed-start road racing is
underpinned by the unwritten etiquette of the peloton, something so complex that not even a Victorian Englishman could
codify it into a booklet of rules. As the French say of cycle racing:
Courir c'est mourir un peu ('To race is to die a little').

Bidlake, a racing cyclist himself and later an administrator at
the heart of British cycling, described the Continental style of
massed-start racing as a 'superfluous excrescence'. He protested
too much, perhaps. The truth is that cycling in Britain never had
the backing of the establishment. Time-trialling was a way to use
the roads for sport without attracting too much attention.

The glittering, lightweight and innovative componentry, the
stylish attire and the cyclists with film-star good looks who came
out of Italy were like rays of dazzling light in post-war Britain.

DOWN
TO THE SEA

by

RALEIGH

Even the colours the Italians painted their bicycles – pearlescent white, yellow, pink, the 'heavenly blue' of Bianchi, said to be the colour of the queen of Italy's eyes – filled the minds of English yeomen with wonder.

The British thought they owned the bicycle. From the day that James Starley patented his Ariel bicycle in 1870 to the mid-1950s, they effectively did (UK output was 3.5 million bicycles in 1955). But you can't own the most popular form of transport in history for ever and the rapid rise in car ownership in the late 1950s meant British cultural perceptions of the bicycle were changing. It was no longer principally a form of transportation. There was now room for new meanings: it could be a toy, as it largely was in America, or an object of desire as it was among the racing-mad Continentals.

'Why not both?' Antonio said, when I asked him about this. 'You have some bicycles that you ride and you have some bicycles on the wall of your house as art, no? Eric Clapton does.'

We'd reached the far end of the factory. In a workshop, mechanics were building up Cinelli bikes, ready to be boxed and sent around the world. Antonio began plucking frames from hooks above his head and components off the workbenches: a

'Vigorelli' track frame, 'named after the great Milanese velodrome known as the "magical ellipse" . . . we sell a lot of these today,' Antonio said; a set of 'Spinaci' bar extensions for racing bikes – 'Spinach gives strength, yes? We were selling 500,000 of these a year when the UCI changed the rules and banned them'; a water bottle with a mint fragrance – 'Smells better than plastic, yes?' There were frame models named after electric guitars and components named after rock bands. I could see Antonio's passion for the bicycle glittering in all these details.

He was most animated when talking about the urban fixed-wheel scene: 'It began in the people's garages. That's important,' he said.

It's not a fashion. It's an attitude. Never has there been such a big crowd of young people studying the heritage of cycling in order to play with the bicycle. They know the history of a particular frame-builder or maybe development of a component. They recognize the car is tired and they've linked the bicycle to real life. They put their personality in it. And they are utilizing high-quality products. We are grateful to cycle messengers. They were the first to live on the bicycle and create a simple, effective, durable machine. This is forcing manufacturers to make better and better bicycles. It means there's more variety in bicycles. The fixed-wheel movement is connected to the rebirth of the bicycle, sure.

Antonio was off now. He began to leap through ideas. He managed to connect John Lennon, rationalist architecture, tattoos, the Provo anarchist movement in 1960s Amsterdam, bootleg music recordings and Le Corbusier with one thread. Come the revolution, he'd be on the barricades, I thought. 'You know the word most people connect to "freedom" in word association or something like this?' he concluded. 'Bicycle.'

We had wandered through the workshop to a table where a dozen bars and stems were laid out. There were simple aluminium bars, around which Eddy Merckx would have felt happy wrapping his powerful hands during his legendary ascent of Col du Tourmalet in the Pyrenees in 1969; and there were futuristic, integrated carbon handlebar and stem units that might have come from the cockpit of Luke Skywalker's X-wing fighter.

'The integrated handlebar and stem is a Cinelli first. For three years, only we make this. Before carbon, all handlebars were round. With aluminium, you have to respect the radius and all the innovation was in the bend. Today the big innovation is in the flat part of the bar. So the ergonomic of the handlebar has changed, dramatically, because carbon can be moulded,' Antonio said. He was holding a non-integrated Ram bar in his hand. His rings clunked against the carbon as he moved his hands around the expansive flat tops of the bar. I suggested there was room to balance a gin and tonic there.

'Why not?' he said. 'Here a place for a cocktail, here your fingers fall naturally round . . . here a place for your thumb . . . when you stay on the hoods, there is space here for this finger, and here, a place where the palm of the hand fits. If you stay on the bicycle all day, it is very comfortable. Touch it, feel it.'

It was the weight of a fountain pen. It felt expensive. It also somehow felt instinctively comfortable. I've suffered from numb hands over the years. It's a common cyclists' complaint, often dubbed 'cyclists' palsy'. It's at its worst off-road, on long descents. The first time I took a mountain bike to Pakistan, I rode off the Shandur Pass (12,450 ft) on a rough, gravel jeep track on a bicycle with rigid front forks. The initial descent off the plateau drops 5,000 ft over 7.5 miles. First my hands went numb – something I was used to – but the alarm bells really started ringing when I realized I couldn't feel anything beneath my elbows, nor could I pull the brakes to stop the bike. When I raised a hand to shake some blood back into it, I fell off the bike. I was still picking grit out of my knees and elbows the next morning.

Even a gentle ride on roads around the shires of England can anaesthetize my hands. I've tried raising the handlebars, lowering the saddle, tipping the saddle fore and aft, not gripping the bars too tightly, gripping the bars more tightly, reducing tyre pressure, most types of gel gloves, thicker grips, cork handlebar tape, gel handlebar tape, and yoga to strengthen the muscles in my lower back. I even gave up smoking. But still, if I sit on a bike all day – road, commuter, mountain bike, it doesn't matter – my hands will go numb at some point, often for some time, and the chances are I'll be woken that night by a dull throbbing in my fingers.

A doctor I once met randomly on a bike ride told me it was carpal tunnel syndrome, the medical term for a compressed median nerve in the wrist. Perhaps. The median nerve, which controls the motor and sensory functions for most of the hand, is in the centre of the base of the palm – a part of the body that is frequently, if not always, under pressure on a bike ride.

There is no doubt that a good fit between bike and rider helps. Brian Rourke was confident that numb hands would be less of a problem on my new steed. And with the Ram bar in my hands, I felt sure I'd stumbled on another part of the solution.

'You have small hands too,' Antonio said, gripping my wrist. 'Then this bar is good for you. See the radius of the bend ... round but a very shallow radius. We call it Varied Radius Concept. It offers more positions but – this is critical – it's easier to reach the brakes. Ten years ago, all the bars went anatomic – you know with a flat spot in the bend – but this forces you into one position only. Then the racers, they wanted round again.'

Brian Rourke had told me about this too. I certainly wanted

a handlebar with a traditional, continuous bend, with a shallow radius. From the side, these bars have a superior aesthetic. Being able to reach the brakes would be a bonus. I hadn't intended to buy a plush and expensive carbon fibre handlebar. I'd come to Milan because I wanted to meet Antonio and see the home of Cinelli. I'd imagined going away with a humble aluminium bar; something Cino might have designed himself. With the carbon bar in my hands, I was wavering. It was exquisite to touch. Yes, they had this bar in the right size for my shoulder width – 42 cm. Oh, and look, here was a beautiful stem in 120 mm – again my size.

Of course, Cino Cinelli would have embraced carbon had he still been alive and applying his inquisitive mind to the bicycle today. And at least the shallow drop of the Ram bar was very similar to the Giro D'Italia model he popularized in the mid-1960s, even if he would have fainted at the sight of the drinks' tray.

3. All Geared Up

Drivetrain

And the bicycle ticked, ticked, ticked.

(Seamus Heaney, 'A Constable Calls')

The Khunjerab Pass (15,500 feet) is one of the highest paved road passes in the world. It's the bleakest point on the Karakoram Highway, which connects the Indus River valley in Pakistan with the Takla Makhan desert in Xinjiang, China. I've cycled over it twice. The second time, it took me a week to reach the Pass from Gilgit, the former Silk Road staging-post at the bottom of the Hunza valley – that's seven days' cycling uphill. There was plenty of inspiration along the way: kids running into the road shrieking, 'Gorah! Gorah! Give me one pen!', the unfettered generosity of the Ismaili Muslims who inhabit Hunza, the egg curries and noodle soups served in the truck stops and the sheer beauty of the mountains. Nonetheless, you need all the physical and mental strength you can muster to cross the Khunjerab Pass on a bicycle.

After the customs and immigration post at Sust, there are 130 miles of no man's land to reach the Chinese post. It's an empty and alienating place. The last 10 miles before the Pass are the steepest. They are hellish. On a cold September day, I wrenched the heavily loaded bike up this road, in bottom gear, standing on the pedals for three hours, extracting every last drop of strength from my legs.

At midday, I reached the Pass – a short, flat section of tarmac edged by snow. I was exalted. It was a pivotal moment: the highest point of my three-year round-the-world ride. I stood there alone, wrapped in all the clothes I had, eating dried mulberries and taking photographs. I'd passed a herd of yaks and a Tajik shepherd near the top. Otherwise, I hadn't seen a vehicle or a person all morning.

As I was packing up, I looked over the edge of the Pass, following the coiling road down into a valley that separated rows of the snow-capped Pamir Mountains. There was a bicycle coming up towards me. I was astonished. Half an hour later, a couple on a recumbent tandem arrived on the Pass. The young Scottish woman at the front, Leslie, was a paraplegic: a climbing accident had left her paralysed from the waist down. She was turning the cranks of the bike with her hands. She was cold and almost mute with fatigue. They didn't linger. I took their picture. They were gone. I was alone again among the white peaks. They seemed somehow smaller.

Physically we are still Stone Age hunter-gatherers. I concede that the modern age of obesity is eroding a truth that has been unassailable for 5,000 years, but for the majority of humankind, 40 per cent of our anatomy is still in our lower limbs. It is a lot for a species that no longer roams across the tundra looking for dinner. It's why the cult of exercise took hold when manual labour declined in the western world. It's why investing in a health club business in China is a good idea today. And it partly explains why the bicycle is the most efficient form of human-powered transport we have ever devised.

Almost alone among human-powered machines, the bicycle uses our largest muscles, the leg muscles, in a near-optimum way.

Today, the drivetrain of a standard bicycle – the handful of components that transfer the efforts of a rider to the rear wheel – comprises the chainrings, the bottom bracket, the cranks, the rear freewheel block with sprockets, the pedals and the chain. It's a highly efficient engine. It's the mechanism that makes the wheels of a bicycle – and my world – go round. It has been argued that the first bicycle equipped with a drivetrain was the brilliant climax to the search for efficiency in tools that began in the Stone Age.

Then, the use of tools first put some daylight between the animal kingdom and us. Nonetheless, we failed to maximize our muscle potential – the most significant source of energy until the Industrial Revolution – for an alarmingly long time. Rowing (anything from a coracle to a galley), tilling, sawing, digging, chopping, shovelling, pumping, lifting – these are all tool-based activities that predominantly made use of hand, arm and back muscles. The principles of cranks have been known about and utilized for millennia, in pumps, lifts and even lathes, but we had a blind spot about driving them with our legs. Nearly all cranked machines were hand-worked. Even one of the world's first submarines, a 50 ft cast-iron vessel deployed by the Confederate army during the American Civil War, was operated by a crew of seven winching an iron shaft attached to a propeller, by hand.

The first ever drivetrain attached to a prototype bicycle was, not surprisingly, hand-activated. In 1821, Lewis Gompertz, a Surrey coach-maker, built a Draisine with an elementary transmission integrated to the steering column: a toothed mechanism at the bottom engaged with a pinion on the front hub. As the rider pulled, the steering column drove the wheel. (Well, sort of.) Around the same time, a London mechanic designed the 'Trivector', a bicycle that carried three people, all engaged in propulsion by hand, while one of them steered by foot. Gaetano

Brianza from Milan built the 'Velocimano' tricycle – the rider
again used lateral hand-levers to propel it.

By the middle of the nineteenth century, the list of great
European minds who had taken a tilt at devising a mechanism
that effectively transmitted the rider's efforts to the driving wheel
of a machine was embarrassingly long: it included Isambard
Kingdom Brunel, Michael Faraday and Nicéphore Niépce, the
photography pioneer. Still, no one recognized that our legs are
more powerful than our arms. The many attempts to build hand-
cranked velocipedes and tricycles would, eventually, put Leslie
on top of the Khunjerab Pass – a wonderful thing. For the rest
of humanity, it was a technological impasse that beggars belief.

The great leap forward happened when someone finally attached
rotary cranks and pedals to the hub on the front wheel of a Draisine and invented the velocipede. Who was the first to do this is
the subject of great debate among bicycle historians. Almost
certainly it was a Frenchman, around 1865. The candidates are
Pierre Michaux, a Parisian blacksmith; Pierre Lallement, a young
mechanic from Nancy who emigrated to the USA and first patented the idea there in 1866; and the Olivier brothers, Marius,
Aimé and René, sons of an industrialist from Lyon and investors
in the Michaux bicycle company. The historian David Herlihy
believes each of them played a part. Whoever it was, humanity
is indebted. It was a breakthrough, not just for the bicycle: here
was a clear path to maximizing the capacity of muscle power in
every human-powered machine.

The addition of cranks and pedals led to the first international
bicycle craze. In 1868, the velocipede spread quickly from Paris
across France, then to Belgium, the Netherlands, Italy, Germany,
the USA and Britain. The machines were made of wrought iron
and wood. They were hard to steer, heavy, inefficient, expensive

and extremely uncomfortable, hence the popular nickname 'boneshakers', but they did at least make use of the right limbs.

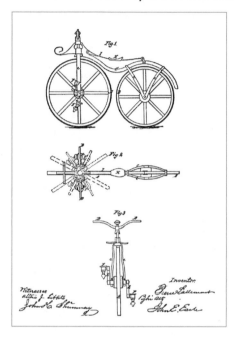

In physiological terms, we get maximum power out of our muscles if they are allowed to function in a cyclical way, and relax for six times longer than they work. It's to do with blood flow. Cycling with regular pedals and cranks, our legs only push on the pedal for a small part of each pedal rotation: about 60 degrees. For the other 300 degrees of the revolution, the main muscles in that leg – hamstrings and quadriceps – are at rest, and able to absorb blood, carrying replacement energy.

So, pedalling matches almost perfectly the optimum ratio between muscle rest and work, which goes some way to explaining why the bicycle is such an efficient human-powered vehicle. Of course, Michaux, Lallement and the Olivier brothers knew nothing of this. It's simply coincidental that human biologists discovered this fact long after the bicycle became popular.

In 1869, during the heady days of velocipede mania, the world's first bicycle race was held, in the wealthy Parisian suburb of St-Cloud. The consequence of this was that people now wanted the bicycle to go faster. A drawback of the velocipede was that there was only one, 'low' gear. In a low gear, the pedals on a bicycle are easy to turn, but you have to pedal fast to get any speed up. In a high gear, the pedals are harder to turn, but you don't have to make them turn so quickly to make the bicycle go fast.

The 'direct-drive' mechanism on velocipedes meant that the front wheel went round once, for every rotation of the pedals. The obvious way to achieve a higher gear was to increase the diameter of the front wheel. Throughout the 1870s, front wheels grew and grew: the upper limit was effectively the length of the rider's inside leg. The largest production bicycles, made popular by professional racers who were reaching speeds of 20 mph, had front wheels of 5 ft in diameter: the circumference of the wheel, or distance travelled per pedal rotation, was 15.45 ft. It was a simple but effective solution to the need for speed. A higher gear also provided a better coupling, or 'speed match', between the human body and the machine. The catch was that machines with large front wheels were difficult and dangerous to ride. In fact, the more the front wheel grew, the further the bicycle drifted from Drais's original vision of a mechanical horse – a democratic machine for utilitarian use.

Mechanics across the industrialized world knew this. In the 1870s, the search for an efficient drivetrain intensified: lever, pivoted-lever, ratchet and front-driving chain mechanisms were all tested, without success. The goal was a system that allowed for a pedalling frequency suited to the capability of the human body to produce power, and to transmit that power from the feet to the driving wheel with as little energy loss as possible – all on a bicycle that was practical to ride. Through popular periodicals like *Mechanics Magazine* and *English Mechanic*, there was a great cross-fertilization of ideas on the subject in Britain. By the end of the 1870s, it was understood that a mechanism connecting the pedals to the rear wheel of the bicycle via a *chain*, and not to the front wheel, which impeded steering and held back the development of gearing, was desirable, if not essential.

With a rear-wheel, chain-drive transmission, gearing up could be achieved by pairing a relatively large front cog (the chainring) with a much smaller one on the rear hub (the sprocket) to multiply the revolutions of the pedals. The advantage was that the wheels could be the same size and smaller, rendering the bike safe to ride. Later, this drivetrain system allowed for both the development of

variable gearing, making pedalling efficient in different conditions, and the one-way clutch called the 'freewheel', which permits coasting. The engineer H. J. Lawson patented the first machine with a rear-wheel, chain-drive in 1879: the problem then was the quality of chains.

The breakthrough came in the form of the steel roller chain, invented and patented by Hans Renold in 1880. Renold was a Swiss engineer who immigrated to Manchester. In 1879, he purchased a small business making rough chains for textile machinery. The company – today an international engineering group operating in nineteen countries – still bears his name. Manufacturing industrial chains remains the core business.

Renold's roller chain, or 'bush roller' chain, was made up of two

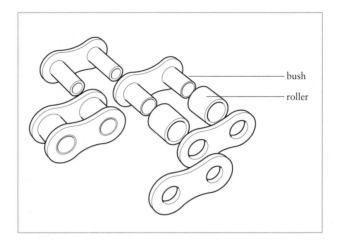

types of alternating links: the inner plates were held by two bushings upon which rollers rotated; the outer plates were held together by pins that passed through the bushings of the inner links. The roller chain smoothed the engagement of the chain with the teeth on the chainring and sprockets. The dramatic effect was to reduce wear and increase efficiency. The most efficient means of power transmission had been found.

In the first half of the twentieth century virtually every form of transport depended on roller chains. One hundred and thirty years after their invention, the concept of roller chains remains central not just to the bicycle but to the transmission of machines used in a plethora of industries across the world. As a eulogy by the Institute of Mechanical Engineers, following Renold's death in 1943, concluded: 'There is hardly a phase of any industry or public works in which the chain is not to be found making an obscure but vital contribution to our welfare.' *Chapeau*, Hans.

Apart from being the daddy of the chain industry, and one of the fathers of the bicycle, Renold was also a philanthropic boss. He started a works canteen at his Manchester factory in 1895 to supplement the poor diet of his employees. He introduced the 48-hour week in 1896 (down from 52) without reducing wages. He welcomed the shop steward movement, gave shares to his employees, introduced profit sharing and established the Hans Renold Social Union. Above all, he respected a good workman. As his son said: 'His whole life was a passion for good work . . . commercial success was of quite secondary interest . . . It might well have been written of him, "Whatsoever thy hand findeth to do, do it with thy might."'

James Starley, the pioneering bicycle manufacturer (more of him in the next chapter) who complained in 1877 that he had to make all his chains himself, instantly recognized the benefits of Renold's low-friction bushings and rollers. Straightaway, he commissioned Renold to make chains for the pioneering tricycles he was working on. James Starley died suddenly in 1881, but his nephew and protégé, John Kemp Starley, continued to experiment with the idea of a chain-driven, two-wheel machine. In 1886, he began manufacturing the Rover Safety. It had a rear-wheel chain drive; it is another late nineteenth-century bicycle innovation that has had remarkable longevity. This was the most significant difference between the safety and every bicycle that had gone before. Nearly every bicycle manufactured since has had a roller chain. The final form in the search for an efficient chain drive had been found: it was fundamental to popularizing the bike.

The chain drive was one of numerous technological innovations that succeeded on the bicycle, only to be borrowed by the automotive industry as it emerged at the turn of the century. The list includes wire spokes, pneumatic tyres, ball bearings, steel tubing and differential gears. Together, they ensured that the quest for an affordable automobile was a realistic goal from the start. Many automobile pioneers were former bicycle mechanics

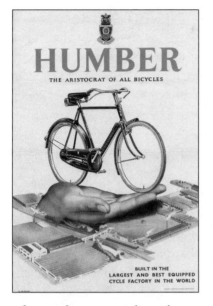

HUMBER

THE ARISTOCRAT OF ALL BICYCLES

BUILT IN THE
LARGEST AND BEST EQUIPPED
CYCLE FACTORY IN THE WORLD

– Henry Ford, Charles and Frank Duryea, William Hillman, William Knudsen and many others cut their teeth building frames, trueing wheels and assembling bikes. Bicycle companies that converted to car manufacturing around 1900 included Bianchi, Singer, Peugeot, Opel, Morris, Rover, Hillman, Humber, Winton and Willys.

The demand for safety bicycles in the 1890s was unprecedented in the history of manufacturing. The industry was forced to adapt quickly to mechanization and mass production to meet demand and the industrial model this created was also part of the economic legacy of the bicycle. Ford and General Motors adopted the model for mass production pioneered by Columbia Bicycles in the USA, Bianchi in Italy and Raleigh in Britain. Ford appropriated the style of management called 'vertical integration'. Assembly techniques and aggressive advertising (the bicycle boom, which coincided with the 'golden age of illustration' saw cycle manufacturers snap up up to 10 per cent of all print advertising in the US) were borrowed directly. The car industry took the reins of campaigning for better roads straight out of the hands of bicycle-makers. Annual model changes and 'planned obsolescence' were cycle industry innovations, though General Motors has since been blamed for introducing the latter practice. The hundreds of bicycle repair shops across the USA were the foundation for the network of motor service stations.

Importantly, the bicycle directed men's minds to the idea of independent, long-distance travel. The two brothers who took the idea furthest were Wilbur and Orville Wright, the 'patron saints of bike mechanics'. The Wright Cycle Company was a storefront bike repair shop and factory in Dayton, Ohio. They applied their understanding of the equilibrium of riding a bicycle to hypothesize about how a flying machine might behave. They mounted wing sections to a bicycle to make comparative tests for lift and drag. They used bicycle sprockets and chains to drive the propellers. Their bicycle repair business entirely financed the research, development, construction and testing that led to the 'Wright Flyer', the world's first powered aircraft.

'In this company, you feel a commitment to foresee the future, but also you feel history all the time,' Lorenzo Taxis, the marketing director of Campagnolo told me. We were sitting in the boardroom above the factory in Vicenza. For several weeks, I'd tried to convince the press office to let me have a tour of the factory. For several weeks, they'd refused. An interview was all I was going to get.

The history of Campagnolo is well known; it's part of road-cycling lore. The company founder, Tullio Campagnolo, was an accomplished amateur racing cyclist. He was competing in a race called the Gran Premio della Vittoria during brutally cold weather on the Feast of San Martino. Different biographies give different dates: 11 November 1927 seems the most probable.

When Tullio reached the top of the Croce d'Aune pass in the Dolomites north of Vicenza, he was leading the race. At that time, racing bicycles still had no derailleurs – the mechanisms attached to most modern bicycles for moving the chain from one toothed sprocket to another, thereby changing gear. It's a French word, with an Anglicized pronunciation – 'de-rail-er' – meaning to throw off course, or derail.

Tullio's bike had two gears, on a double-sided rear hub with two sprockets – commonly a high fixed gear for the flat and a low freewheel for climbing. To change gear, you had to remove the rear wheel and flip it round. First the wing nuts that secured the wheel in the drop-outs had to be loosened.

In the ice and snow on the top of the pass, with fingers frozen numb, Tullio struggled to loosen the heavy wing nuts and flip his wheel round. A score of his rivals swept past, no doubt jeering under their frosted breath. On completing the race, Tullio is reputed to have said: 'Bisogna Cambià qualcossa de drio' – 'Something needs to be done about the rear.' He meant it.

On 8 February 1930, Tullio Campagnolo patented the quick-release skewer – a steel skewer within a hollow hub axle with a nut at one end and a lever with a cam to fasten it at the other. It was simple and brilliant: it operated in all conditions. Instead of unscrewing nuts to remove a wheel, you simply pulled open a lever. It has remained fundamentally unchanged for eighty years. Today the quick-release skewer is a universally standard fixture on almost every bicycle manufactured. Every day, across the globe, tens of thousands of cyclists turn their bikes over to remove a wheel – to repair a puncture or slip the bike into the boot of a car. With their fingers round the levers of the quick release, they silently honour the memory of the inventive guru, Tullio Campagnolo.

The quick-release skewer was the first of some 135 patents the great man registered. Eighty years later, that spirit of innovation is still strong at the company he founded; it's why I couldn't get past the boardroom.

'We own many patents. Every day, we are working on new products,' Lorenzo said. 'There is a lot of technology in the road-racing bicycle, and a certain jealousy of what Campagnolo do. This forces us to keep the know-how within these walls. We are a privately owned company, and Mr Valentino Campagnolo doesn't let the media enter the secrets of the company.'

I had read that, during the boom in the 1890s, Albert Pope of Columbia Bicycles, then one of the largest manufacturers in the world, refused to let any journalists into his factory in Hartford, Connecticut, for the same reason. I mentioned this.

'Yes. And if you enter Ducatti or Ferrari today, it is the same,' Lorenzo said.

In a way, it's a marketing problem for us. A company like Campagnolo should really advertise the brand through its technology, by letting the consumers see how the products they are passionate about are produced. But we can't. More important to us is innovation: it's part of the DNA of the company. It always has been. Today the innovation is in electronic gear-shifting, in bearing technology, in refining carbon fibre to reduce the weight of our componentry. We have to innovate . . . to stay alive.

For the first thirty years of the twentieth century, racing had little impact on the development of the bicycle. This is a curious anomaly: during the 1890s and then from the 1940s until today, the technological development of the bicycle has been inextricably linked to the sport through the testing and marketing of new products. The improvements between 1900 and 1930 – butted tubing, aluminium components, early derailleurs – came from the benign world of cycle touring. In fact, competitive sport held the evolution of the bicycle back. The racing community spurned any developments that might somehow detract from the purity of their sport. The view was that human valour should be allowed to prevail over technological advantage.

Henri Desgranges, the editor of a French sporting daily, developed the idea of the Tour de France in order to outsell a rival newspaper. He wanted stories of machismo in forbidding mountains, adversity in extreme weather, heroism and the crucifixion of men. He wasn't interested in gadgetry. Desgranges said: 'Variable gears are only for people over forty-five. Isn't it better to triumph by the strength of your muscles rather than by the artifice of a derailleur? We are getting soft.' When the French component company Mavic produced the first aluminium wheel rims, Desgranges prohibited the use of them too. The perfect Tour, he often said, would have a perfect winner if only one man survived. The circulation of his newspaper flourished. Desgranges' control over the Tour ended in 1937.

Tullio Campagnolo manufactured parts in a workshop behind his father's hardware store, before registering the company and inaugurating production of the quick release in 1933. In the same year, he patented a prototype derailleur mechanism, using a sliding hub and rods attached to the seat stays. This was slowly modified and improved over the course of more than a decade until, in 1948, Gino Bartali used the *Cambio Corsa* ('race changer') derailleur in the mountain stages, en route to victory in the Tour de France. In 1950, a parallelogram derailleur with an extended jockey cage – something we'd recognize today – was revealed at the Milan bicycle show. It was as complex a piece of componentry as the bicycle had ever seen, but it meant that no-fuss gear shifting was suddenly a reality. Everyone wanted one. Only pro racers and amateurs with deep pockets could afford them.

In the early 1950s, the bond between Campagnolo and the elite of road racing was sealed with a string of victories for riders using Tullio's components: Hugo Koblet in the 1951 Tour de France; Fausto Coppi in the 1950 Paris–Roubaix, the 1952 Giro d'Italia and Tour de France double, as well as in the 1953 World Road Race championships. Both riders were using *Gran Sport* derailleurs.

Campagnolo, now employing over 100 people, began to re-appraise and manufacture pedals, seat posts, cotterless cranksets, aluminium hubs and chainwheels. Business boomed. By the 1960s, the company diversified into motorcycle hydraulic and cable disc brake components, magnesium wheel rims for super-cars like Maserati, and even aerospace parts, including the chassis for a NASA satellite launched in 1969.

A staggering amount of research and development in close association with professional riders ensured that all the ideas to improve the bicycle introduced by Tullio reached a point of unrivalled reliability, before the product was sold on the market.

Tullio Campagnolo died in 1983. Plaudits and awards – the Stella d'Oro by the Italian Olympic Committee, the Cavaliere del Lavoro, Italy's highest business honour – had been heaped on him by then. In a lifetime of inquiry, he re-appraised many aspects of the bicycle, established the most coveted name in the components industry, and helped claim ownership of the racing bicycle for his country. Eddy Merckx gave a eulogy at the funeral: 'I tell it to you in bad Italian, maybe, but with an Italian heart because, thanks to you, there is a piece of Italy with your name on all the bicycles of the world.'

Until recently, the history of the bicycle was murky. Only following the rigorous academic work of a small collective called the International Cycling History Conference has it become clearer. Prior to the late twentieth century, the true technological progress of the machine, together with the hands and minds involved, was muddied by the proprietary claims of several industrial nations. Such jingoism was at its worst before World War I. Germany claimed Baron von Drais's 1817 'running machine' was the first bicycle, though it was really only a prototype. The French avowed that de Sivrac had invented the bicycle in 1791, but it was a non-steerable machine. In England, it was maintained that the bicycle, in fact, began with the Rover Safety in 1885. Even the Scots staked their claim with the story that Kirkpatrick MacMillan, a Dumfriesshire blacksmith, added reciprocating cranks to a velocipede forty years before that. There was no consensus. Then, in 1974, an Italian literary historian, Professor Augusto Marinoni, chucked a big stick in the spokes.

Marinoni revealed to the world a sketch of a bicycle by Leonardo da Vinci. The sketch was found in a folio of drawings from Leonardo's studio known as the *Codex Atlanticus* and dated to 1493. On the reverse of a drawing of a military fortification, between a caricature and, bizarrely, promenading penises, there was a sketch of a bicycle complete with two similar-sized, in-line wheels, an elementary steering system, cranks, a saddle and a chain connecting a chainwheel to a sprocket on the rear wheel. All the fundamental elements of the bicycle were there. Its proportions were strikingly close to the machines of today. Here was proof that Leonardo had invented the bicycle, a bicycle with a drivetrain no less, at least 300 years before de Sivrac, Drais,

Michaux, Lallement, MacMillan, Starley or any of the other pretenders. Here was indisputable proof that the bicycle was Italian. The only people to whom this was *not* a knee-buckling revelation were the Italians themselves. Deep down, the *Tifosi* had known all along.

According to Marinoni, monks at the Abbey in Grottaferrata near Rome discovered the sketch during a restoration project of Leonardo's work. Reams of drawings from his studio had been glued into albums in the late sixteenth century, one of which was named the *Codex Atlanticus*. The monks had painstakingly unstuck the pages, revealing a vast array of new drawings covering an extraordinary sweep of not-yet-invented technology. And there was the bicycle. The sketch became familiar worldwide when *The Unknown Leonardo*, a scholarly tome on the restored manuscripts, was published in 1974.

Leonardo's engineering ideas are striking; many were centuries ahead of Renaissance technology. He drew sketches of a helicopter, a parachute, load-lifting devices, a wooden 'car' driven by springs with geared wheels, triple-barrelled cannons, a glider, a portable bridge and scuba gear. That a vision for the world-changing invention, the bicycle, first appeared in the frenetic corridors and trammelled passages of the brain of one of the greatest engineers in the history of mankind, in 1493, appealed to bike fanatics everywhere. Marinoni's timing was good. In 1974, the oil crisis – the OPEC embargo on oil to the USA because of support for the Israeli military during the Yom Kippur War – was in full swing. Bicycle sales were booming and the number of bike fanatics grew daily. The bicycle sketch was published again and again, in newspapers and cycling and engineering periodicals. It probably made it on to dish towels at some point. Quickly, it became an accepted part of the history of the bicycle.

There was one problem – the sketch was a hoax. It may even

have been a deliberate fraud, added to the volume during the lengthy restoration of Leonardo's papers, to claim proprietorship of the bicycle for Italy. Foisted upon a gullible world, it worked. In fact, it worked so well that no one considered it appropriate or necessary to investigate the provenance of the sketch for twenty years. A little detective work led Dr Hans-Erhard Lessing, a German transport historian, to conclude the sketch was a forgery. Upon examination, it proved to be a poor forgery; an amateurish doodle on top of an original sketch of two geometrical circles with some lines. We'll probably never know who the forgery was by. Professor Marinoni was probably no more than naive in propagating it. One of the monks, then?

To me, this is the most appealing story. I'd like to think that a cycling-mad monk in the Laboratorio di Restauro, part of the venerated library within the tenth-century Abbey of Santa Maria di Grottaferrata, was bored one day. The *Codex Atlanticus* comprises 1,119 pages of drawings and writings dating from 1478 to 1519. The monks had been working on restoring it for five years. On this day, say sometime in 1972, our cycling monk holds up sheet 133. The backside of two pages, which are stuck together, is translucent. He spies the faint outline of two geometric circles; two wheels, perhaps. He holds the paper closer to a light that scarcely breaches the gloom of the medieval library. He squints again, harder. 'Yes, yes, there's definitely a set of wheels. Could there be a frame too?' he thinks. 'And components? Could it be a bicycle? No, wait, if it's a bicycle, that means . . . a miracle.'

The abbot coughs loudly in another aisle. Our monk returns from his reverie. Carefully – for this is his expertise – he peels away the backing page of folio 133. The pages were hurriedly stuck together by Pompeo Leoni, the sculptor who acquired Leonardo's drawings in the late sixteenth century. There on the page are two circles with some unexplained markings. There is no bicycle. The disappointment is great, almost as great as the disappointment that no Italian has won the Giro d'Italia for three years, nor the Tour de France for seven years. It's 1972, remember: a nadir for the *Tifosi*. It's Merckx, Merckx and Merckx out there.

Idly, our monk starts doodling – just a few spokes. Thinking of the great frame-builder, Faliero Masi, 'the tailor', in his workshop under the Vigorelli velodrome in Milan, he pencils in a frame. Then the face of Cino Cinelli appears to him, and he draws a handlebar. He's merely filling in the blanks. 'Of course Leonardo invented the bicycle,' he says to himself. He starts drawing faster, with purpose – cranks, pedals, and sprockets. The winged emblem of Campagnolo flits through his mind. 'What does it matter? Everyone knows the bicycle is Italian. It's as Italian as the dome of St Peter's.' A saddle, and it's done. He glues the pages back together again. A bell rings. 'Ah, lunchtime,' he says.

'Italians like design, colours, shapes. We care a lot about the aesthetics of the bicycle,' Lorenzo Taxis said. 'This is the part of the bicycle you could really say Italy has ownership of. The care in the details, it's part of the Campagnolo way. We are a product-oriented company. Our products sell at the top of a pyramid of a mature industry. The bicycle has not changed for a long, long time. Only the performance has improved. So the development of all new products is followed by Mr Valentino Campagnolo himself. He believes that if you can bring to the market outstanding products that also look beautiful, then the business takes better care of itself.'

Campagnolo are today best known for their 'Gruppi' or group-sets – a set of components made by the same manufacturer, designed and machined to work together. The first Campagnolo Record '*gruppo*' was marketed in 1958. Prior to groupsets, quality bicycles were commonly equipped with components cherry-picked from several different manufacturers: brakes by Mafac, crankset by Chater-Lea, pedals by Barelli, and so on. The debate about the pros and cons of the groupset has simmered among cyclists since 1958. The argument in favour is that components are manufactured to work efficiently together, while providing a unitary look to a bicycle. The argument against is that the big component makers have reduced consumer choice and success-fully reserved for themselves a larger share of the market.

At the beginning of this project to put my dream bike together, I vowed to eschew the groupset. I sketched out in my mind a bike with perhaps a Tune chainwheel, Specialités TA cranks, brakes by Ciamillo, a Stronglight chain and Campagnolo derailleurs. When I mentioned the plan to Brian Rourke he winced: he actually physically recoiled, like someone receiving a low-voltage electric shock. When he'd recovered, he carefully made the case for a groupset, or at the very least a drivetrain comprising matching components. The compatibility issue was significant: 'You could have yourself a right headache, Rob,' he said. More important to Brian, though, was how the bike looked. It was OK to go off-piste with the hubs and the seat post. Even the brake calipers could be from an alternative manufacturer. But the drivetrain, derailleurs and integrated shifter/brake levers were sacrosanct, on purely aesthetic grounds. Brian had been right on so many other things. I chose to trust him.

Once the decision to buy a *gruppo* was made, I knew precisely what I wanted: Campagnolo Record. The first Record *gruppo* in 1958 comprised a chainset, bottom bracket, hubs, seat post, headset, front and rear derailleurs and pedals. Today, it's a more refined list: chain, chainset, cassette, front and rear derailleurs, levers and brakes. It's a hideously expensive kit. For me, it would be a massive indulgence. I'd add to it my own pedals.

The name Record runs through the entire history of cycle sport in the second half of the twentieth century. The word alone is venerated; it has a touch of ju-ju about it. The Record groupset, through all its different guises and materials, has forged an association with victory that is unparalleled not just in cycling, but in sport. The thirty-six Tour de France victories between 1958 and today and the twenty-six wins in the Giro d'Italia between 1968 and 1994 give some idea how dominant Campagnolo Record componentry has been.

Like many, I've admired and coveted Record components for a long time. When I was 12 years old, a boy in the neighbouring village had a duck-egg blue Peugeot racing bike with a Campy Record groupset. The components were hand-me-downs from his Dad but that boy buffed them up like he'd paid for them with his own blood. The bike was so sumptuous it hurt me just to look at it. Thirty years later I can close my eyes and still see that bike, with its shining drivetrain, against a stone wall, beside the well, outside the churchyard.

There was no point putting Campy on my round-the-world bike. I went for a Shimano groupset then, in the knowledge that finding replacement components in remote places would be much easier. I've waited and waited to drop (a lot) of cash on Campagnolo Record components. My time had come.

'Happy Christmas,' Lorenzo said, pushing the box across the table. 'The cardboard weighs more than the components.' With a few strokes of a Stanley knife, the box was open. Each component was individually packaged. Lorenzo commentated as I began to pull them out: bottom bracket cups – 'English standard size'; the rear derailleur – 'So much technology in here'; the crankset – 'Ah, the sexiest piece of them all. Cranks are 170 mm. Compact chainrings. This is correct for you, yes?'; brakes, integrated shifter/brake levers, cassette – 'Eleven speed.

The best.' And the chain that would supply the kinetic sound-track to all my future rides.

It was like being given a box of jewellery. I was overawed. Then I remembered I wasn't being given it at all. I was buying the *gruppo*. I winced. It was, as Will, my oldest cycling companion and best man, had said: 'a classic mid-life crisis purchase'.

4. The Lateral Truth, So Help Me God

Wheels

I'll ride this here two-wheeled concern right straight away at sight.

(Banjo Paterson, 'Mulga Bill's Bicycle')

Gravy was tall, like a Redwood. Even hunched over his bike snaking across the car park, I could tell. 'Hey, must be Rarb,' he said, adding 'arrrb' to my name in his lolloping Californian accent. He offered me a hand the size of a tennis racket. Then he broke a smile that could span the Golden Gate Bridge: 'Welcome to Fairfax, Marin County. Thanks for making the trip. Better come on in. See if we can fix you up some Gravy wheels.'

Everything about Gravy was big – even his reputation. From the beginning of this project, I asked everyone I spoke to: 'Who builds the best bespoke wheels?' Many named their local wheel-builder, out of innate loyalty. Some put themselves forward. A few even named rival wheel-builders with whom they'd fallen out long ago. But the deeper I got into the bike world, the more I asked, and the more one name kept coming up: Gravy.

Flying to the West Coast of America to get a pair of custom wheels made is extravagant by any measure. I simply can't do that, I first thought, even though I knew I could pick up the headset for my bike on the same trip. What finally swung it was a telephone conversation with Gravy: 'Awesome if you could make it, man,' he said. 'We'll get you some beautiful wheels, for sure. We'd also get you set up riding down Mount Tam on Repack. That's where the shop is, right here at the foot of Repack. Maybe Charlie Kelly and Joe Breeze are around. What would you say to riding down Repack with Charlie and Joe?' I dropped the phone.

If you're not a mountain bike fanatic, you wouldn't know that Repack is the most famous off-road trail in the world. It's the birthplace of the mountain bike. Here, in the late 1970s, a bunch of hippy bike bums turned the American hillbilly cruiser bike into the all-terrain bicycle – the form of the bicycle that would blaze a technological trail through the late twentieth century. It was the most significant innovation in the design of the bicycle since John Kemp Starley's Rover Safety. It had huge ramifications: as one bicycle historian wrote: 'The mountain bike saved the bicycle industry's butt.'

The 1974 oil crisis had prompted a boom in bicycle sales in America, the first significant spike since the 1890s. But by the late 1970s, the industry had stuttered to a halt. The mass-market, ten-speed racing bikes had hard tyres and even harder saddles: only experienced cyclists extracted any pleasure from riding them. The machine had unintentionally drifted a long way from the utilitarian, user-friendly 'people's nag' envisaged by Starley.

What began as a cottage industry in the garages of Marin County slipped, in 1981, into mass production: the Californian company, Specialized, manufactured 500 Stumpjumpers in Japan. They sold out in three weeks. Today, there's one in the Smithsonian National Museum of American History. The big players in the market, all of whom initially snubbed the 'ugly bikeling', took note. It was the beginning of a gold rush that revitalized the industry in America. In just a few years, the mountain bike went global. In 1985, 5 per cent of US bicycle sales were mountain bikes. A decade later, it was 95 per cent. In 1988, 15 per cent of the 2.2 million bicycles sold in Britain were mountain bikes. By 1990, it was 60 per cent. In 1996, mountain biking became an Olympic sport.

The new machine touched a nerve. The mountain bike was comfortable to ride. It evoked nostalgia among Americans for a style of bicycle popular in the middle of the twentieth century. It perfectly caught the imagination of the baby boom generation. They all wanted one; suddenly, a practical bike was affordable again.

If Repack was the birthplace of the mountain bike, then Charlie Kelly and Joe Breeze were the midwives. I'd been reading about them for twenty years. They are legends. The chance to ride Repack with them was too good. I dug out my passport.

'C'mon, Rarb. C'mon on in to my laboratory. Take a look around while I get fixed up,' Gravy said. The 'laboratory' was Gravy's workshop, tucked away at the back of a cavernous bike shop called the Fairfax Cyclery. The walls were densely packed with memorabilia – signed photos, cycling shirts, over-sized cranks – from Gravy's thirty-year association with the bicycle. Steve 'Gravy' Gravenites grew up in Mill Valley, down the road from Fairfax, when the sport of mountain biking was somewhere between conception and birth. He raced mountain bikes for ten years, followed by a decade on the road ('visiting all the world's unknown ski resorts,' he said) as a leading race mechanic or 'wrench'. He worked for international mountain bike teams like Yeti, Schwinn and Volvo-Cannondale, as well as for individual national and world champions such as Tinker Juarez, Myles Rockwell and Missy 'the Missile' Giove.

When Gravy reappeared with coffee, I had my head inside his old toolbox or 'race case' as he called it. It had been round the world at least ten times and had the stickers to prove it. Common tools were on the top level; the heavy artillery was down below.

Only Gravy's wheel-building expertise surpasses his wrenching credentials: 'Three decades I've been building wheels, two for money. I don't reckon I've built ten thousand wheels yet, but I'm gettin' close,' he said. Before manufacturers made complete wheelsets in factories, he built wheels for entire mountain bike teams. His philosophy – to tailor the wheel to the weight, height, riding style and riding conditions of each rider.

You can have a bicycle without derailleur gears or brakes: it's called a 'track' or 'fixed-wheel' bike. Track riders have to ride them; regiments of urban cyclists love to. If pressed, you can even have a bicycle without a bottom bracket, sprocket, chain, chainwheel, cranks and pedals. Take away all this and you've stripped the bicycle back to the bare essential parts of the Draisine.

Take away the wheels, though, and you do *not* have a bicycle. All you have is a wooden bench, or a set of tubes, welded together in an odd shape that's no good to anyone. Wheels are fundamental. This much is reflected in both the definition of and the etymology of the word – 'bicycle'. *Chambers Twentieth Century Dictionary* definition is: 'a vehicle with two wheels, one before the other, driven by pedals'. 'Cycle' comes from the Greek *kyklos* meaning 'circle' or 'wheel'.

The machine was not called a 'bicycle' from the beginning, though. Words like this grow. They don't issue, at the touch of an inventor's hand, from the machine itself, and immediately fit. No, people won't accept any word. The long list of appellations in English pre-dating 'bicycle' includes Draisine, pedestrian-accelerator, dandy-horse, dandy-charger, hobby horse, pedestrian-curricle, boneshaker, velocipede, ordinary and high-wheeler. The term 'bicycle', probably coined in France in the late 1860s, first appeared on a British patent in 1869 and was adopted after 1870.

As the Flemish novelist Stijn Streuvels wrote, 'Has any machine ever become so popular, so widespread in so short a time, and have we ever had more difficulty in finding a name for it?'

Each nation, of course, gave it a name in their language and went through a similar selection process. In Holland, they tried '*rijwiel*', '*trapwiel*' and '*wielspeerd*', before settling on '*fiets*'. The French took a bit of Greek and a smidge of Latin and bolted them together to form '*vélocipède*' ('fast-foot'). The word was too sluggish for something so brisk, so it was shortened to '*vélo*' and preferred to '*bicyclette*', '*bécane*' and '*bicloune*'. *Vélo* is a good word: if I shut my eyes and let the 'vvv' vibrate on my lips, I can summon a sensation of laziness, pedalling along on a summer evening. I also like, again for purely aural reasons, '*rad*' (German), '*rothar*' (Irish), and '*podilato*' (Greek). But the real word, the utilitarian, living word, the word borrowed with slight modifications by dozens of languages and understood by a substantial majority of the world's population is – 'bicycle': two wheels.

Installed on an orange couch in the window of the bike shop, Gravy carefully took the front and rear hubs that I'd brought with me. They were Royce hubs, manufactured by Cliff Polton in Hampshire, England. I'd been led to Royce by reputation, just as I was to Gravy. Brian Rourke first mentioned them – 'bomb-proof,' he'd said – and then, as when you learn a new word, Royce started to pop up everywhere. I saw the understated 'R' laser-etched on to the hubs of hand-built wheels; Polton popped up in magazine articles about the dying days of British engineering excellence; and people who had heard about my project randomly emailed me to extol the beauty of Royce components. Polton made components for Nicole Cooke when she was a junior champion. More famously, he made the hubs for the bike Chris

Boardman rode to break the world 'Athlete's Hour' record (the record that must be attempted on a conventional bike with spoked wheels, drop handlebars and round frame tubes, and different from the 'Absolute Hour' or 'Best Human Effort') at the Manchester Velodrome in October 2000.

Royce hubs are simple and beautiful. The spindles, machined  from aerospace-grade titanium, are guaranteed for the 'life of the original purchaser'. The aluminium hub shells are CNC machined and expensively finished. In fact, the hubs look like jewellery. I knew I needed to look no further. But there was one hitch: when I rang to place an order, Polton told me he'd sold out of 32-spoke, Campagnolo-compatible rear cassette hubs. No more would be made for several weeks (he was on a bee-keeping course), and certainly not before my trip to California. But he did have a 28-spoke, Campag-compatible rear hub. What did I weigh? What was the bike for? 'Oh, you'll be fine with that,' Polton said.

Gravy inspected the hubs at close range, over the top of his glasses, like a gem dealer eyeing diamonds:

I'm noticing titanium axle, medium flange width, beautiful machine work going on here, nice chamfer . . . no holes or nasty edges that might crack in the future, a real nice high polish that seals the metal. Titanium freehub body on the rear hub, much stronger than aluminium, that's good. The bearings feel super smooth. Great set-up. These should last you a long, long time, Rarb. This'll be the first pair of Royce hubs I've ever built up. Awesome. Now, what tyres are you planning on running on this machine?

I already had the tyres: they were Continental Grand Prix 4000s. I'd been to the factory to see them made a few weeks earlier. I chose Continental simply because they had never let me down. Riding round the world, I always tried to run two Continental *Town and Country* tyres on Mannanan. In extremis, I'd settle for one on the rear. They were the toughest tyres by, well, a town and country mile.

The small, medieval town of Korbach in central Germany is dominated by the factory (located on Continental Street) in the way towns in Lancashire were by mills in Victorian times. A vast red-brick chimney rises to meet the sky. On the morning I arrived, a Stygian grey haze hung over the buildings. The air was cold. The factory was dark. I felt like I'd walked into a scene from a Sherlock Holmes novel: not inappropriately – Arthur Conan Doyle was a keen cyclist and Holmes boasted of being able to identify 'forty-two different impressions left by tyres'.

The sunshine piercing the gloom came in the shape of Hardy Bölts, my guide for the day. Straight-backed, tall, lean and tanned, he was another specimen exemplifying the physical benefits of life spent on a bicycle. Hardy had raced as a pro, both on the road and the mountain, before joining Continental. Flashing a fine set of white teeth, he clasped my hand and swished his ID card to open the gates.

'You know the nickname for Korbach?' he said. 'Rubber Town. And how about that smell, the smell of heated rubber? It never goes away. Like a bicycle saddle, you get used to it after a while.'

The people of Korbach have had long enough to get used to it. Continental, now one of the largest global suppliers to the automotive industry, employing 150,000 people in eighteen countries, began making bicycle tyres in Korbach in 1892. It's a manufacturing record that spans almost the entire history of the pneumatic tyre.

John Boyd Dunlop, a Scottish veterinary surgeon resident in Belfast, invented the pneumatic tyre in 1888. A doctor had advised cycling for the health of his 9-year-old son, remarking that the activity would be all the more beneficial if the jarring from the rough granite cobbles on the city streets could be reduced.

No doubt the entire cycling population would have then concurred. Comfort was something no one expected or sought from cycling. During the boom in velocipedes – known with good reason as 'boneshakers' – tyres were made of solid iron. By the time the Rover Safety bicycle was introduced in 1885, tyres were made of solid rubber strips and tacked or glued to the wheel rim. It was an improvement on iron; even so, a simple bike ride could still rattle a man's molars free.

Dunlop tacked sleeves of linen to the wooden wheels of his son's tricycle and inserted crude, inflatable rubber tubes with a non-return valve and filled them with compressed air. It was like having a flexible cushion strapped to the wheel. It worked. Dunlop christened the word 'pneumatic', patented the idea and began small-scale production in Dublin. The first advertisement appeared in the *Irish Cyclist* in December 1888: 'Look out for the new Pneumatic Safety (bicycle). Vibration impossible.'

At first the tyres were expensive and quick to puncture. Though the reduced rolling resistance clearly made the bicycle faster, the bulging 'bladder-wheels' or 'pudding tyres' as they were called, met with hilarity and derision in Ireland. In 1889, an Irish journalist rode a pneumatic-tyred machine from Dublin to Coventry, one place where the bicycle had never been a laughing matter. In a year, every racing cyclist in the country had pneumatic tyres. After two years, the Dunlop factory relocated to Coventry. Six years after that, the business was floated for £5 million.

Dunlop himself never profited greatly; he died in 1921 with under £10,000 in his estate. In fact, he hadn't invented the pneumatic tyre, though he believed he had. Another Scot had patented the idea (for carriage wheels) in France and the USA in 1846. Nevertheless, Dunlop's pneumatic tyre came at a critical point in the development of road transport and played a crucial role in the birth of both the motorbike and the automobile. For the bicycle, it was the last piece of the jigsaw. The steering system meant you could balance on two wheels in-line; the diamond-shaped frame and same-sized wheels made the machine strong and safe to ride; the drivetrain made it efficient. And, finally, Dunlop made the bicycle comfortable. It was perhaps a development as important as the arrival of the Safety itself. The pneumatic tyre made the bicycle popular.

'We start here,' said Hardy Bölts, 'with natural rubber.' Huge carpets of thick rubber were being sucked on to rollers above our heads and heated with chemicals to make a black, gloopy porridge. It was like something out of Willy Wonka's Chocolate Factory. As the porridge was squashed flat between rows of great drums, it spluttered and popped like a witch's brew. The noise was terrific. Close to the rollers, it was hot. The workers with heavy gloves and beads of sweat edging their moustaches, grunted at us.

'Twenty-four hours a day, seven days a week, 358 days a year, these machines are rolling. For one week only each August, everything stops,' Hardy said.

Further down the production line, multiple layers of nylon thread were spinning off spools and being pressed and bonded into the hot rubber sheets: 'The finer the nylon, and the higher the threads per inch or TPI, the better the tyre,' Hardy said as we watched the finished, rubberized tyre casing being stored in giant rolls at the far end of the factory.

The sensory assault was over. On the second floor, where the bicycle tyres are manufactured, the environment was more equable. The first thing I noticed was how many employees were female.

'There are many steps in the production of high-quality bicycle tyres that just can't be done well by machines,' Hardy said. 'Many of the jobs are fiddly and sticky. They involve small parts. Women have smaller hands . . . and they are more skilful.'

The most delicate part of the process was the assembly of the tyre itself. I watched a woman roll a strip of casing material on to a wheel and add two beads of steel wire. The machine then folded this single ply over twice, before she added an anti-puncture strip and, lastly, a piece of tread. The ends were sealed together. A sticker to show who had made it was added and the tyre was hung on a hook behind her. The whole operation took forty-five seconds.

'If you or I try this,' Hardy said, 'then everything is flying through the air. Every tyre has to be made like this, by hand. It is checked again and again. Every tyre has to bring you safely down an Alpine pass at 90 kph [55 mph].'

A high-speed 'blow-out', when the tyre bursts spectacularly with the sound of a gunshot, is one of the things road cyclists fear most. If you are dropping like a stone down a mountain road, you can be thrown from the bike, leaving the gods to decide your fate. The one dramatic blow-out I had that still gives me flashbacks was in the Fergana Mountains in Kyrgyzstan. I was coming down from a pass on a gravel road, on a loaded touring bike. When the hairpins finished, and the road opened out before me, I let the brakes go. At full tilt, the front tyre – a cheap Chinese-made tyre I'd bought in the market in Kashgar – blew. The bike slid briefly, then the handlebar jack-knifed and I was off. Somehow, the bike was propelled into the air. As it came down on top of me, the teeth of the chainrings scalped the side of my head.

A few hours later, I reached a farm on the road – the first settlement I'd seen all day. Blood congealed with dust covered the side of my face. My shirt was shredded. Looking like a cross between a cage-fighter and a Sadhu, I leant my bike against the gate and walked up the path. Children and women scattered, shrieking. The farmer, a barrel-chested Kyrgyz man with taut, mongoloid features, appeared from the shadows with a pistol at the end of his stiff arm. I tried a few words of Russian. No reply. Then his eyes flicked past me to the gate, and my bicycle. The pistol arm fell limp. The leathery brown skin on his face re-set to a broad grin. Ten minutes later, I was eating kebabs and yoghurt as his wife sponged blood from my head. I had the bicycle to thank for my salvation: it was the last time I would ever grace it with a cheap tyre.

The earliest pneumatic tyres had to be glued on with rubber solution. At the end of the 1880s in France, the young owner of a struggling rubber factory, Edouard Michelin, was astounded to learn from a cyclist with a puncture that he had had to wait an entire night for the glue to dry, after he'd repaired the inner tube and re-stuck the casing. Soon after, Edouard introduced a detachable tyre – the 'changeable'. Any cyclist could now repair a puncture, without glue, in fifteen minutes.

Edouard's brother André was the marketing brain behind the business. Having treated the French professional cyclist Charles Terront (more of him in the next chapter) to a bibulous luncheon in Paris in September 1891, he had the famous racer sign a contract to ride the Paris–Brest–Paris race on patented Michelin changeables. Terront won, by eight hours. André strolled among the 10,000 fans at the finish on the Champs-Elysées, handing out brochures that read: 'We have every reason to believe that the bicycling public will say of our tires, "An improvement? – No, a revolution!"' In truth, the revolution was Dunlop's, but the changeable soon developed into the 'clincher' – the type of tyre most of us ride today. The steel beads with which the woman had assembled my Continental tyres, became standard. Like Dunlop, Michelin became a household name.

Remarkably, the tubular style of tyre that has to be glued on is still used today, mainly by professional track and road cyclists. Of course, the pros have a team of mechanics to deal with the messy business of fixing them to rims and repairing punctures. Tubulars are favoured for their marginally better shock absorption and road feel. 'And they are a little faster,' Hardy said. He should know – he rode in the Tour de France and the Vuelta a España on Continental tubular tyres.

We watched a woman use a sewing machine to finish a tubular tyre. She carefully stitched the inner tube inside the rubberized cloth casing, blew it up, checked it over by eye and hooked it on the rack behind her. It was, again, highly sophisticated handwork. 'It's a small but important part of the business. We want to keep the pros happy. Perhaps this tyre is for Mark Cavendish's bike,' Hardy said.

The final part of the process to manufacture my clincher tyres was vulcanization, the technique invented by the American Charles Goodyear in 1843. Natural rubber is sticky; it deforms

under heat and becomes brittle when cold. By heating it together with sulphur, the rubber becomes durable, elastic and
stable, rendering it waterproof and winter-proof. Without the
vulcanization process, we'd still be riding on bicycle tyres made
of iron.

'See the raw tyres – they are your tyres, Rob – they are going
into the oven. They have no form and you could pull apart the
tread and the casing with your hands. But after three minutes inside
the machine, at a temperature of 160°C [320°F], the vulcanization
is complete and the tyres are indestructible,' Hardy said.

We were standing at the end of two rows of sixty machines
that took one tyre each. They were closing and opening continuously, at different times, belching steam. Each one contained
a negative mould with different tyre treads. Three men walked
up and down the rows, placing raw tyres into the maws of the
machines and hauling vulcanized tyres out. One of the men
nodded at me. We walked down to meet him. He spoke to Hardy
in German and handed me a pair of industrial gloves. 'OK,' Hardy
said. 'Any minute now you can pull your two tyres from these
ovens. They'll be smoking hot, and ready to ride.'

Placing the hubs on the couch between us, Gravy flipped open a
clipboard. Both hubs were 28-hole: both wheels would have 28
spokes. All things being equal, the more spokes a wheel has the
stronger it is. But more spokes do mean more weight and increased
aerodynamic drag. It's about finding a balance, then. The conservative approach, for the ultimate in reliability, would have
been a 32-spoke rear wheel for me, Gravy explained, but as I
weighed only 165 lb, we could easily build in strength to com-
pensate, with the rim and spokes we chose.

Step one was choosing the rims. Clearly I wasn't going to be
allowed the lightest rims. I wasn't going to choose them anyway.

I hadn't come to California to get a set of super-light special race-day wheels: I'd come for a set of everyday riding wheels. My primary concern was strength, not weight.

Even so, the one place on a bicycle you don't want to carry unnecessary weight is in the wheels. As wheels are accelerated round as well as forward, the mass of rotating parts is doubled, for the purposes of calculating acceleration. So, if a 22 lb bike has 13 lb in fixed mass and 9 lb in rotating mass, the effect will amount to 31 lb. It's partly why high-quality wheel rims are made of lighter materials like aluminium and carbon, not steel. It's also why the quality and attributes of rims, spokes and hubs can have a greater impact on the performance of a road-racing bicycle than any other components.

'I'm gonna steer you towards a DT Swiss rim. DT Swiss have been in the business a long time and I know how history makes you Brits feel kinda warm,' Gravy said.

Ah, the comfort blanket of history. DT Swiss began drawing wire at a mill on the banks of a river outside the town of Biel in 1634. The wire was used in the manufacture of shirts for soldiers in the French army. Biel, the cradle of the watch-making industry, is famous for micro mechanics and the manufacture of highly specialized tools and machinery. It's the sort of pedigree that makes me feel, yes, warm.

The rims – model RR 1.2 – weighed around 18 ounces. They were made of aluminium, but they looked robust. The spoke bed was reinforced and, Gravy explained, the whole rim was coated in helicopter rotor paint, which adds to the longevity.

The weight and strength of any rim is, of course, only relevant within the total assembled structure: put another way, you can buy the most expensive rim in the world, but if the wheel is badly built, it's no good to you. As to colour, I had the choice between black or silver – a no-brainer for me. Scratch black paint and a new wheel rim looks old; scratch silver and it's silver underneath.

The RR 1.2 was not a cycling fashionista's choice. It wouldn't bring tears of envy to the eyes of the 'weight weenies' – the sub-cult of road cyclists who obsess about the weight of every component. But the wheels would, Gravy assured me over and over, last a long, long time.

People were ambling in and out of the shop while Gravy and I talked. Some had business to conduct. Others simply came in to chat, over the dub reggae, with one of the mechanics – about bike parts, routes or that evening's music gig across the street. It was as laid back as a beach bar in Antigua and it said much about the strong, friendly community that exists around the bicycle in Fairfax.

The previous evening, I'd wandered around Fairfax, a town of 7,000 resolutely individual people and home to Van Morrison in the 1970s. I watched all the smiling cyclists spilling into the town centre from the surrounding pine-covered mountains, at the end of their evening rides. I ate Vietnamese food at the farmers' market in Bolinas Park, listening to a busker playing classical guitar. I had a smoothie in the organic supermarket and a beer in 19 Broadway, listening to a blues gig. In Peri's Silver Dollar Bar, the dance floor was full of people jiving to swing music. The manager led me into the ladies' toilet – a shrine devoted to Elvis. 'You gotta meet the guy who did this, right?' he said. 'He's called Rudy Contratti. You can't miss his place. He's gotta a picket fence made out of old skis and a 14-ft blue marlin stuck to his house.'

I invited myself into Rudy's, passing beneath the 14-ft blue marlin. We had a beer ('I drink it cold, Rarb. Can you handle that?' Rudy asked) and a tour of his fleet of fully restored, art deco bicycles from the 1930s to the 1950s. The bicycles were museum pieces. The house smelt sweetly of marijuana. I thought

Fairfax might be the kookiest town I'd ever idled into. It was a town of big hats and tattoos; a town of healthy people who held your eye and smiled spontaneously; a town where purple trousers had never quite gone out of fashion. I asked Rudy if people in Fairfax were happy. 'Let's put it this way,' he said, 'ain't nobody here lost money in the Bernie Madoff Ponzi. And everyone rides a bicycle.'

'For sure everybody rides,' Gravy said. 'I never owned a car.' For every mile of paved road, there are 15 miles of dirt road in Marin County. There are half a dozen groups going out riding from Fairfax every day: you can join any one. As a kid, Gravy used to ride all over Mount Tamalpais, which is how he met the guys at the birth of mountain biking in the mid-seventies.

'I was the first little punk on the scene with all these dudes wearing logging boots and jeans and getting all sideways on their bikes and going super fast,' he said. 'You know, they had this gonzo attitude and they were so into it, it was infectious. I got involved.'

The other side of Gravy's life is no less intriguing. His Dad is Nick Gravenites, a Blues legend, upon whom John Belushi's character in *The Blues Brothers* is based. His Mum was flatmate and stage-clothes designer to Janis Joplin. As a baby, Gravy lived in a flat above the Grateful Dead on Haight Street, San Francisco, navel of the hippy movement that gave counterculture to the world. I asked about the move from the all-night crowd to the keep-fit crowd.

'Yeah, the bicycle saved my life all right,' Gravy said. 'And building wheels is like tuning guitars: every spoke has to be humming perfect.'

Sapim have been manufacturing spokes in Belgium for over ninety years. Apart from a few tools, the company makes nothing but spokes and the small nuts or 'nipples' that secure them to a wheel rim. Expertise, innovation, strict quality control, specialization, the ability to adapt to technical developments in other parts of the bicycle and a small loyal workforce: these are the characteristics of Sapim. They also happen to be characteristics common to the best bicycle component manufacturers from the birth of the industry until today. I'd read all about Sapim. The company bears the stamp of quality.

Their spokes have been 'a staple' in the world of professional racing for decades, according to Lance Armstrong's ex-team director and confidant, Johan Bruyneel, a former pro rider himself. Perhaps more than anyone in the modern sport, Bruyneel knows that success in road racing is about scientific precision. Love and hate in the Technicolor peloton, doping, courage and the depth of human suffering make better newspaper headlines, but the reality is – you win with the best components. Armstrong won all his seven Tours on Sapim spokes.

Sapim make a great range but Gravy recommended the traditional round, double-butted stainless steel wire spokes. They are lively, springy, and less prone to breakage with a little fatter surface area for threads, which increases the strength of the ends. Gravy opened a lever-arch file and extracted a spoke from a plastic sleeve. In his tennis racket paws, it looked like a spoke from a child's bike. I could see it was 'double-butted', with a middle section that was thinner than the ends: I knew this increased elasticity and strength while reducing failure from fatigue.

The front wheel of a bicycle is symmetrically dished, it carries less weight than the rear and it doesn't have to bear any torsional load. This means you can get away with lighter spokes. Gravy recommended the standard Race model for my front wheel: 2 mm in diameter at the ends, down to 1.8 mm in the centre.

As the rear wheel has to be stronger than the front, Gravy

suggested something different: the Sapim Strong spoke. It, too, was double-butted, but 2.3 mm at the ends down to 2 mm in the middle. On a 28-spoke rear wheel, it would provide a great balance between 'feel' and durability. And it fitted with the overall philosophy of the bike – an everyday riding bike, built to last.

Most spokes are made from stainless steel: it's strong and doesn't corrode; it has good fatigue resistance and it's easy to cut smooth, strong threads for the nipples. You might find titanium or ornately shaped carbon fibre spokes on very expensive wheels. But, like oval and flattened spokes – designed to reduce wind drag, but susceptible to torsional twist – these are really for racers who value weight and performance over durability and cost. Most cyclists require round, stainless steel, and double-butted spokes. Gravy knew well what I needed. And in selecting different spokes for my front and rear wheels, I was getting the full benefit of the made-to-order service.

The big question was whether the Strong spokes would fit through the holes of my Royce hub. Rolling a spoke between his thumb and forefinger, Gravy placed it carefully through a hole in the flange. With a 'tch-ik', it dropped into place.

'Oh, yeah. Look at that. That's awesome.' His face broke into another Golden Gate smile. DT Swiss RR 1.2 rims, Sapim spokes – Strong in the rear and Race in the front, standard brass nipples. It was a deal. We high-fived.

'I'm going to hit the trenches now and build some wheels. And you're heading up the mountain . . . I've just seen Joe Breeze walk in with an original Breezer mountain bike and you . . . are . . . in . . . for . . . a . . . treat. I wanna go! You're gonna go do Repack, with original Repack riders, on original Repack bicycles. You're gonna be mobbed. You're gonna have smoking, flaming, burning wheels of fire. Yeah!'

★

I can clearly remember the first time I rode a mountain bike. Like the first time I listened to a Sony Walkman, it was a defining moment. I was walking down a steep street at university, behind the students' union, in 1987. Coming up the other way I saw Mark, a design student; we worked on a magazine together. I knew the hill well. Climbing up it on my battered ten-speed racer was an out-of-the-saddle wrench that scraped cigarette tar off the floor of my lungs and made my calf muscles bulge like chicken drumsticks. Despite the gradient, Mark was pedalling freely and keeping pace with his mate, who was on foot. They were having a conversation. I'd read about mountain bikes but I'd never sat on one – they took a while to get from the dirt trails of Marin County to the Georgian streets of Bristol. The first time I did, I wanted one.

The story of the invention of the mountain bike might be the most intriguing chapter in the entire history of the bicycle. It's certainly the most unlikely. Around 1973, several young Californians began modifying pre-World War II, balloon-tyred, American single-speed 'cruiser-bikes' in order to ride them downhill, at full tilt, on footpaths – for fun.

The distinctive feature of this new style of cycling was that it was *off-road*. The aged bikes, nicknamed 'clunkers', were neither designed nor built for the task, but they were cheap and dispensable. Riders hammered them until they broke, then bought another one. One of the most coveted models was the Schwinn 'Excelsior': the relaxed frame geometry, long fork rake and high bottom bracket gave this model a small design advantage over others.

Soon, the riders began to modify these clunkers. Non-essential parts were stripped off. New parts, cannibalized from every kind of two-wheeled vehicle, were added. Tyres got fatter and more knobbly, frames were strengthened, brakes were improved, stronger brake levers and quick-release seat posts were affixed, cranks got longer, chainsets got better; in time, derailleur gears and thumb shifters appeared. All these features and components had been invented previously; it was just that no one had put them all together, on one frame, with the specific aim of blitzing downhill, off-road.

The greatest concentration of riders actively modifying clunkers was based around Mill Valley, San Anselmo and Fairfax, small communities in Marin County, north of San Francisco, around the foot of Mount Tamalpais. Here, fortune brought together a young, energetic group. There were no more than half a dozen key players, but it was a critical mass. They were athletic, inquisitive and highly competitive. They included: Charlie Kelly – rock band roadie, writer and general outlaw – who was the charismatic organizer; Joe Breeze – decorous local boy and racing cyclist, who grew up riding over Mount Tam, could build frames and had access to his father's machine shop; Gary Fisher – a Category 1 competitive road racer and mechanic with a sense of inquiry and plenty of chutzpah; Tom Ritchey – a successful road racer and full-time frame-builder when he graduated from high school. None of them went to college. They shared a passion for bicycles. Otis Guy, Larry Cragg, Wende Cragg and Alan Bonds were part of the same crowd of friends and also influential. In the hands of this small coterie of inquiring cyclists, the clunker evolved into the mountain bike.

Over the years much has been made of the fact that they were a gang of dope-smoking, hippy bike bums. They may have used the early clunkers to 'tend north country cash crops' as Gary Fisher wrote, and they were 'a bunch of people who didn't have to go to work every stinking day', as Charlie Kelly said. But the invention of the mountain bike was not like a cartoon from *The Fabulous Furry Freak Brothers*. It was dynamic.

At the heart of the story was Repack – a dusty, often

precipitous, off-road footpath that drops 400 m in just over 3 km (1,300 feet in 2 miles) with an average gradient of 14 per cent, down the side of Pine Mountain, a foothill of Mount Tamalpais, finishing near Fairfax. The young mountain bikers had been riding it for a couple of years, during which time one question simply wouldn't go away – who is the goddam fastest? There had to be a race. The gang met on 21 October 1976. It was a time trial. Riders set off from the start at 2-minute intervals. Alan Bonds won. He was the only rider who didn't crash. His dog, Ariel, came second.

There were only ever twenty-five Repack races: remarkably few for the legend that grew out of them. The last race was in 1984. They were organized and publicized by Charlie Kelly. Joe Breeze won the most races. Gary Fisher holds the course record. No more than 250 people got to race the course, yet Repack was critical.

On the dirt and gravel, over bare rock and gullies, ruts, roots and boulders, at average speeds of over 25 mph, down slopes of up to 20 per cent and round

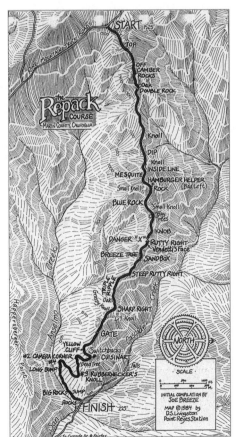

reverse camber corners, blind turns and switchbacks, the mountain bike evolved, broken bike by broken bike.

'We were always pushin' the bike. No question about it,' Joe Breeze said. In a typical Repack race, half a dozen bikes would fail. Riders went home and immediately started repairing and modifying their machines, in the hope of a better run next time. For some, this tinkering turned into a lifetime's work. Joe Breeze now runs a company that manufactures 'transportation' bicycles; Tom Ritchey and Gary Fisher both established global brands that bear their names.

The name of the race, 'Repack', even came from the act of fixing a bike. 'Back in the day, coaster brakes – you know the kind you operate by pushing backwards on the pedals – were the most popular,' Charlie Kelly said. 'You packed the brake hub with grease to keep them smooth. In a race, the grease heated up so much it just boiled out, leaving a contrail of black smoke behind the bike. When you got to the bottom, it howled so hard you had to go home and *repack* that hub again with grease.'

The three of us were wheeling our bikes up Repack on a balmy, late summer afternoon. The ground was 'crackle' dry. Sunlight illuminated the pillows of dust that our boots scuffed up as we climbed. Charlie was pushing a 1941 Schwinn – a quintessential clunker. Joe had one of his original 'Breezer' bikes. He designed and hand-built ten in 1977–78. Made from nickel-plated, cro-moly aircraft tubing, in a diamond shaped frame and fitted out with Phil Wood hubs, TA cranksets, Dia-Compe cantilever brakes and BMX style unicrown forks, Breezers were the first ever purpose-built mountain bikes. It was a landmark. Joe kept one. The remaining nine are either in private collections or museums. I was riding a bike built by Joe in the late 1980s. Technologically it was sound, but it had little character compared with their bikes.

'To say it was a quantum leap from this,' Charlie said, halting

to wave a hand the length of his clunker, 'to that Breezer there kinda understates quantum leaps.'

Both Charlie and Joe were dressed in the clothes they would have ridden in thirty years ago: boots, Levis, denim shirts and caps. Joe did have a pair of leather gloves on – the single concession to protective wear.

'Heck, no one ever had a helmet. All considered there were few injuries. Lots of accidents, but few injuries. I broke that.' With the bike hooked against his hip, Charlie held up both hands like he was stopping traffic. 'Right hand, left hand. Notice the large deformity? Broken thumb. Happened right up there at Hamburger Helper, nasty corner.'

'What happened?' I asked. 'Hand on the ground?'

'Nah, that was everything on the ground. And hitting it very, very hard, and laying there for a while because I didn't want to discover what was broken and then realizing if I don't move soon, somebody's going to ride right over me.'

A hallmark of the Repack races was the competitiveness. Laying in the dirt, Charlie might have remembered his own call to arms prior to one of the races: 'If you crash and break a few bones, wait for the first-aid crew, unless you're blocking a good line: if so, then try to drag yourself off to one side. If you see somebody down on the course and bleeding, stop and give help – unless you're on a real good run.'

As we walked, Charlie and Joe frequently stopped to explain, with verve, how you rode different bits of the course fastest. I learnt the best lines through the corners – 'on the inside here, right on the tangent of the apex' – where to un-weight, and places to stamp on the pedals to 'steal a second before you jump on the brakes again at the next corner.' Though it had been thirty years since they were riding it regularly, every rock, branch and rut was recalled. In the heyday, Joe made a map of the route and Charlie once took a photograph every 50 feet, as *aide-mémoires*, so that 'in the moment, you were totally dialled in'.

We hadn't quite reached the top of the path where the race began before Charlie suggested we turn and take a crack at the descent: he's not a man you'd ever say 'no' to. Joe, in his fifties and a paragon of good health, could hardly wait to get going down. He was practically scraping the dirt with his boots, like a Spanish fighting bull. With a quick tug on his gloves and one deep breath, he was off.

There was no more ceremony to Charlie's departure. He dragged a big boot off the ground and was gone. I could hear the roaring of the knobbly tyres, scrabbling to keep a grip on the mountain, as they both plummeted out of sight. I swallowed a lungful of the glitteringly clean air. I looked down the trail, past the huckleberry bushes and the poison oak, across the valley to the slopes of chaparral crowned by the peak of Mount Tamalpais (2,571 feet). I tried to mentally photograph the vista: 'Top of Repack, August 2009. Ready to burn.'

I've owned a mountain bike for over twenty years. The list of hills and mountain ranges I've cranked up and hammered down includes the Brecon Beacons (where I started riding and now live), the Mendip Hills, the Grampians, MacGillycuddys Reeks, the Karakorams, the Hindu Kush, the Alps, the Dolomites, Snowdonia, the Cascade Range, the Remarkables, the Great Dividing Range, the Barisan mountains, the Western Ghats, the

Kopet Dag, the Tien Shan, the Pamirs, the Zagros mountains, Jebel Liban, the Himalayas, the Dinaric Alps and the hills of North Harris.

I was once sent by a newspaper to write a feature on the Scottish downhill mountain biking course in the shadow of Ben Nevis, before a World Cup event. I was placed in the charge of Stu Thomson, a 22-year-old national champion. In the gondola on the way up, Thomson told me how the last journalist he'd escorted (from a competing publication) had fallen off at the first corner and refused to get back on his bike. Was every journalist, he wondered, this wet? Professional rivalry got the better of me and I listed the mountain ranges I'd known on two wheels.

I, too, fell off at the first corner. One moment, I thought 'this is magical'. I could see for miles down the glen over the crooked finger of Loch Eil to the Atlantic Ocean. Before I'd finished the thought, my coccyx was bouncing down a boulder.

When I caught up with Thomson, having kissed the granite of Scotland again twice, I was rictus-faced, flushed with adrenalin, battered in body parts I'd forgotten about, numb in the hands, terrified and on the verge of being sick. 'Yer grabbin' the breeks,' he said. 'Ya cannee grab the breeks. Ya cannee have a doubt.'

Charlie and Joe were long gone. The mountain was silent. I had no doubts. I pointed the bike down the fall line, released the brakes and stood on the pedals. Within seconds, I was dropping like a stone. Coming into the first corner, I dabbed the brakes. The bike jolted like a dying man receiving a bolt of electricity to the heart. No photo or film of the original Repack races comes close to exposing the thrill of riding it. It was very fast. Around the second or third corner, they were waiting for me.

'Pretty sketchy, huh?' Charlie said. I wondered if they had found it scary 'back in the day'.

'It was always scary,' Charlie replied, 'but that was why you did it, right? If it was safe . . . it wouldn't be fun.'

Joe's eyes revealed how much fun he was having. He took off again. Charlie and I rumbled along behind. We came round a left-hand corner, with reverse camber and a big drop off the right side of the trail, called 'Tripple Ripple'. Like a motor racing circuit, many of the course features had names. We'd passed 'Rubberneckers' Knoll', 'Camera Corner', 'Breeze Tree', where Joe had once taken a wrap, and 'Vendetti's Face', where 'Mark Vendetti left behind a lot of his face,' Charlie said.

When we reached the first big switchback, I asked about the speedway style cornering I'd seen on old footage, in the film *Klunkerz*. Joe explained: 'With the old brakes, the drum brakes, which were kinda like non-brakes, you'd come into the turn and you'd be using your bike to scrub off some speed. You come into it and you un-weight, kick the rear end out, and you're comin' through kinda sideways. The front wheel's still turning so you're holding the line. Your inside foot's down. The other foot is on the pedal. And if you're really good, there's no hands on the brakes.'

Most of the Repack races were held between 1976 and 1979. 'There was never a schedule. It was just something we did when we felt like goin' out and doin' it,' Charlie said. The races stopped when Charlie stopped organizing them. In 1979, a TV crew came to film the race; a rider fell and broke his arm; he sued the TV company and lost; Repack's cover was blown; the public authority who owned the land now knew about the races; no one wanted to take responsibility for organizing a race where people got sued.

Like the best rock stars, Repack died young. The job was done. The cross-pollination of ideas among the riders, and the hammering the course inflicted on every bike, had led to the Breezer, the first purpose-built mountain bike. Several other cottage industries in Marin County were also making mountain bikes by 1979. Repack had given the mountain bike publicity, creating a market for the bikes. The fun was over. It was time for business.

We were near the finish now. 'You'd be flying on your 50-pound iron by here,' Charlie said.

The coaster brake would've overheated. It'd be howling. There'd be rocks sailing out of the trail here and there. You're just tryin' to keep that straight line into the last corner and past the boulder that was the finish line. Often enough, that's where the concentration lapsed. Either that or it was too tempting not to lock up the brake and get all sideways and finish off with a big Franz Klammer slide.

Joe's eyes flickered with energy again. He hopped on the pedals and tore off. As Charlie and I rounded the last corner and saw the boulder, a great chute of dust flew up, accompanied by the roaring of denim through dirt. Joe had gone in for a Franz Klammer slide and hit the deck. Charlie was laughing before he put his bike down.

'Sorry I explained that earlier, didn't I? I did explain that to you,' he hooted, hitching his jeans up and pointing at Joe who was bent double, staggering about with his arms wrapped across his belly, howling with laughter too.

The spoke pattern of a wheel is determined by how many times each spoke crosses adjacent spokes between the hub and the rim. Radial spokes do not cross at all: they project straight out from the flange – the raised part of the hub where the spoke holes are – to the rim. Crossed or tangential spokes project more or less on a tangent away from the flange: between the hub and the rim, they may cross over or under one, two, three or even four other spokes. Generally speaking, the more times spokes cross, the more they pull on each other, and the stronger the wheel.

So, a loaded touring bike that's being ridden by a big man on dirt roads across South America would have three- or even four-cross spoke wheels: his only concern is durability. My round-the-world bike had three-cross wheels, front and back, all the way. At the other end of the spectrum, a featherweight racing bike ridden competitively by Nicole Cooke would most likely have a radial-spoked front wheel and a rear wheel with two-cross spokes on the drive (or gear) side and radial spokes on the non-drive side: her concerns are weight and aerodynamics.

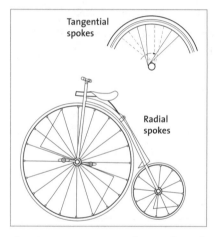

The reason the spokes on the drive side of the rear wheel should be crossed is because radial spokes cannot transmit torque – a force applied in the form of a twist rather than a push or pull. The chain applies a rotating force to the hub when you pedal, twisting it relative to the rim: to transmit this to the wheel, and go forward, you need to have (or at least it's much better to have) crossed spokes on the drive side.

There are more elaborate spoke patterns, such as crow's feet (radial and crossed spokes combined), Spanish laced, snowflake and offset radial. Some of them do look beautiful, but they have no practical advantage over standard, cross-spoked patterns. It's just somebody pimping their ride.

Gravy wanted to build my wheels tangent-spoked and three-cross. To ensure this was possible, he first had to measure the internal diameter of the rim, the thickness of the rim at the nipple hole (you'd imagine that these dimensions are standard but Gravy explained they can vary from one 'extrusion' or batch of rims to another), the width of the hub, the distance from the outside of the flanges to the edge of the hub, and the hub flange diameter (the distance from centre to centre of the spoke holes). He typed the figures into a spoke-length calculator on the Sapim website.

Before computers, Gravy did the calculations using tables. Getting the spoke length exactly right is important because the next step is to cut the spokes to that length and re-thread them – using the trusty old Phil Wood spoke cutter, a dense, grey hunk of manually operated machinery in the corner of the workshop. If the spokes are cut to exactly the right length, you get the maximum amount of thread in the nipple, and they're less prone to breakage. You can't ask a machine that builds wheels to do all this, I thought.

Ting – up came the spoke length on the computer screen. 'OK. The 'puter, it says we can build both wheels three-cross. Three cheers for your Mr Starley.'

James Starley is the greatest British inventor you've never heard of. He's a colossus of the self-taught entrepreneurial, manufacturing cadre that ensured the industrialization of Britain was a *revolution*. Cycling historian Andrew Ritchie described him as 'probably the most energetic and inventive genius in the history of bicycle technology'.

Starley was born to agricultural labourers on a farm in Sussex in 1831. At 15, he left a note on the kitchen table – 'Dear Ma sorry can't stand it any more going to London will write soon Jim' – and ran away from home. Clearly, he was in such a hurry, there was no time for punctuation. His head was a hothouse of mechanical ideas from a young age. Working as a gardener in Lewisham, his natural aptitude for mending clocks, sewing machines and other devices, as well as for inventing things, caught the attention of the eminent marine engineer John Penn.

Penn introduced Starley to the businessman Josiah Turner, and in 1857 the pair moved to Coventry, historically the centre of clock-making in Britain. It says much about the times that two entrepreneurs would leave London and move to Coventry to make their fortunes. They established the Coventry Sewing Machine Company and Starley invented and patented many kinds of sewing machines (several innovations remain standard today), before Turner's nephew returned from Paris in 1868 with a velocipede – the early form of the bicycle then causing a stir in France.

Edward Ward Cooper, a company employee, described in his autobiography the arrival, 'in the sacred precincts of the office a "thing" from France . . . We all gather round. Mr Turner, our manager, "Ole Starley", the mechanical genius, myself and a few awestruck officials . . . Yes, there the thing stood; no one ventured to touch it.' When Starley did first touch it, he lifted it up and complained about the weight.

The velocipede or 'bicycle' as the machine began to be known, fell on fertile ground in Britain, a country with a strong metalworking tradition. Even so, it was a bold decision by Starley and Turner to apply their efforts to a nascent industry. In Starley's hands, improvements to the crude French 'boneshaker' followed quickly. In 1870, he patented the all-metal Ariel bicycle (jointly with William Hillman, whose name lived on in the car industry). In the same year, France went to war with Prussia, suspending the manufacture of velocipedes across the Channel. The Ariel marks the true beginning of bicycle manufacturing in Britain. It put the country in the vanguard of bicycle technology for eighty years and earned Starley the moniker 'Father of the bicycle industry'.

'To demonstrate to the bicycling fraternity the qualities of the new bicycle,' a contemporary account noted in 1871, Starley and Hillman rode Ariels from London to Coventry, in a day. They 'mounted their machines just as the sun was rising' and, 'pedalling bravely, they reached Mr Starley's residence just as the clock of St Michael's struck the hour [of midnight]'. It was a remarkable feat – 100 miles on primitive roads. Starley was 41 years old and he weighed 196 lb. Both men didn't get out of bed for three days, but the ride attracted public interest.

The Ariel was advertised as 'the lightest, strongest, and most elegant of modern velocipedes'. It wasn't hyperbole. The name itself – perhaps a play on the word 'aerial', or borrowed from Shakespeare's sprite in *The Tempest* – hints at how lissom the machine was. It went on sale in September 1871, at £8 for the cheapest model. One of the first customers was James Moore, the famous racing cyclist.

The Ariel quickly became the benchmark for the new wave of 'high-wheeler' or 'ordinary' bicycles. Hollow steel tubular frames, improved bearings, pivot-centre steering, slotted cranks, a brake, solid rubber tyres and a rear-step for mounting all became

standard features as the machine developed. Yet one innovation in particular distinguished the Ariel as a landmark in the history of the bicycle: the front wheel.

The wheel is one of humanity's greatest inventions. Its history is the story of civilization. Though the wheel was probably invented earlier, the first wheeled vehicle we can roughly date – 3,200 BC – was found in southern Mesopotamia (modern Iraq). It was a solid wooden dish with a hole in the middle for an axle to pass through. The next evolutionary step came some 1,500 years later. Skilled Egyptian carpenters learnt how to craft wooden wheels using radial spokes, making their chariots lighter and faster. From then until the beginning of the nineteenth century, the wheel hardly evolved at all. Of course, wheelwrights grew more adept at their craft and the materials developed, but structurally the wheel remained the same. In our age of almost daily technological advances, it seems incredible that something so fundamental could remain effectively unchanged for so long.

The first hint of a development came three millennia later when the tension spoke was patented in 1802. An iron-spoked wheel was patented in 1826 and carriage-makers experimented throughout the nineteenth century with metal spokes, as an alternative to wood, but without success. Eugene Meyer, a

Parisian cycle manufacturer and master craftsman, was probably the first to develop a decent suspension or 'tension-wheel' for a bicycle in 1869, featuring individually adjustable spokes. But it took a man of ingenuity and vision, James Starley, to see the potential of this type of wheel and put it into production. The 'lever-tension wheel' that was standard on the Ariel changed the bicycle for ever.

The wooden wheel with rigid spokes had served humanity well. In the late 1860s, it was constructed in largely the same way as it had been for millennia: rigid spokes were secured to a wooden rim and held firm by an iron hoop which had been heated and allowed to contract as it cooled.

It worked simply – the ground pushes up on the rim, which pushes up into the spoke, which pushes up into the hub. The hub pushes back down on the spoke. The spoke is said to be in *compression* under load, because both ends of the wooden spoke are being pushed towards each other. If a vehicle was stationary, you could cut away every spoke, except for the one or two at the bottom, and the wheel would not collapse; the thick, heavy wooden spoke is strong enough to support the load.

The tension-wheel works differently: the wire spokes are stretched tight when the wheel is made. Every spoke pulls on the hub simultaneously, but they are in balance, so the hub and rim stay put. Thus, every spoke plays some role in supporting the hub at all times and the hub is effectively 'hung' from the top of the rim rather than entirely supported by the bottom spoke. When a load is applied – you sit on a bicycle, for example – the ground pushes up on the rim, which pushes up on the bottom spoke or spokes, but the tension already in those bottom spokes *decreases*; they become less stretched or looser, while all the other spokes remain unchanged. If a vehicle was stationary, and you cut away every spoke except for the one or two at the bottom, the wheel would collapse: one or two thin, light, wire spokes are not nearly strong enough to support the load.

The first advantage of the tension-wheel was that it was more comfortable: in the pre-stretched wire spokes, there is an element of suspension. Tension spokes absorb road shock much better than rigid spokes. The fundamental advantage, though, was the weight saving – a critical matter in respect of wheels, as we've seen. Think of the weight you could hang from a single wire spoke; then think of the wooden spoke you would need beneath that same weight, to support it.

Starley's and Hillman's 'lever tension-wheel' with radial spokes replaced the wooden wheel with thick, rigid spokes, for good. The Ariel was about a third lighter than the wooden-wheel velocipedes that had gone before. Crucially, this innovative wheel was so strong and light, the diameter could now increase. Strong and reliable wooden wheels simply couldn't be built with a diameter over 1 m (40 inches), but tension-wheels grew bigger and bigger, ushering in the age of the high-wheeler or ordinary bicycle, which directly preceded the rear-wheel chain-driven safety bicycle.

High-wheelers didn't have gears: they were direct drive, so, for every turn of the pedals, the wheel went round once. The easiest way to 'gear up' a bicycle was to make the drive-wheel larger. Thus, the length of a rider's inside leg now determined the upper limit; the largest production high-wheeler had a front wheel diameter of 1.5 m (about 60 inches). This was not the limit, though; with new materials tension-wheels have grown and grown. In fact, the recent addition to the London skyline, the London Eye, is a tension-wheel.

Starley continued to experiment with spoke technology. In 1874 his efforts culminated in the 'tangent-spoked wheel', the method by which Gravy was going to build my wheels. It was Starley's greatest achievement. The tangent-spoked wheel followed the same load-bearing principles as the tension-wheel, but with cross-spokes the wheel was braced; and the force driving it was more efficiently transferred from pedal to rim. Spokes were angled; adjacent spokes were angled in almost opposite directions; the tangent on one side balanced the tangent on the other; spokes were laced for strength; each spoke could be individually tensioned, and the wheel could be easily adjusted to stay radially true (the rim is perfectly circular) and laterally true (the walls of the rim are perfectly flat, with no wobbles).

Starley continued to innovate, designing a popular chain-driven tricycle with differential gears, and the masterly Salvo quadricycle, which entranced Queen Victoria. He died in Coventry on 17 June 1881.

Nearly every bicycle wheel made since 1874 has been built using the tangent-spoking method. The innovation would later be borrowed in the motorcycle, automobile and aeroplane industries, among others. It remains the best method for building bicycle wheels to this day.

We now know that the high-wheeler or ordinary (it only became known as the 'penny farthing' once its popularity was declining in the late 1880s) was a brief vogue that led the bicycle down a technological cul-de-sac. It had two important consequences for society, however.

The expansion of the railway network across Britain in the 1840s had killed the stagecoach business, leading to the neglect of the once excellent turnpike road system. The pioneering work of Thomas Telford, the civil engineering giant known as 'the colossus of roads', and John McAdam, who invented the first road-surfacing process, was long forgotten. In fact, in the 1870s, roads were worse than they had been at the beginning of the century. Great lumps of stone, as well as mud and ruts, were the norm. For cyclists, accidents were common. As the Earl of Albemarle, president of the National Union of Cyclists, wrote: 'The only obstacle that I know of to the use of cycling becoming universal in this country, is that year by year the roads seem in many parts of England to be getting worse and worse.'

The athletic and adventurous young men who rode high-wheelers formed clubs, with captains, uniforms, badges and buglers, who served to protect their members from the pot-holes – the bugler rode in front sounding the alarm when he came across a crater. The clubs also campaigned to improve roads. By the mid-1880s, the biggest club, the Cyclists' Touring Club, had 20,000 members. It was a powerful force. Through it, the bicycle became a major factor in the rebirth of the idea that roads were a national concern.

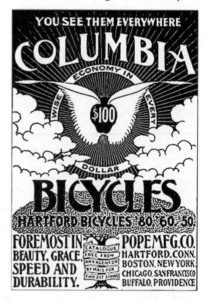

In America in the 1870s the roads were even worse. Quagmires in spring and dust tracks in summer, they were known as 'gutshakers'. For Colonel Albert A. Pope, who began manufacturing Columbia high-wheeler bi-cycles in 1878, improving roads was the key.

Pope involved himself in every aspect of the bicycle. He established an annual trade show, organized races and financed lawsuits against municipal regulations that prejudiced cyclists. He founded *The Wheelman* magazine and distributed it gratis. He offered prizes to the medical profession for pro-cycling articles. Most significantly, Pope spearheaded the powerful 'Good Roads Movement'. He had a section of tarmac laid in downtown Boston, to show how smooth roads could be. He made a donation to establish a course in road-building at the Massachusetts Institute of Technology and he launched the League of American Wheelmen in 1880, which organization immediately took up the demand for better roads.

In the 1880s, the advancing roadworthiness of the high-wheeler seems to have unlocked the minds of young gentlemen to the possibilities of travelling by bike, as the mountain bike would do again, a century later. C. Wheaton, a manufacturer in Covent Garden, London, produced a 'Map of the British Isles for Bicycle Tourists' and rented bicycles by the month. Clubs set off to tour France where, from the mid-1870s, the bicycle industry had begun to flourish again. In 1875, Albert Laumaillé rode a 54-inch Coventry Machinist bicycle 1,127 km (700 miles) from Paris to Vienna. In 1882, Ion Keith Falconer, a record-breaking amateur cyclist, Scottish aristocrat and missionary, rode from Land's End to John o'Groats, completing the 1,600 km (994 miles) in thirteen days.

Thomas Stevens, an American immigrant from England, departed from San Francisco Bay on a black-enamelled Columbia 50-inch 'Standard' high-wheeler, on 22 April 1884. He rode around the world. It took him three years. He pedalled through England, Continental Europe, the Balkans, Turkey, Iraq and Iran, where he wintered as a guest of the Shah. Expelled from Afghanistan, he took a ship from Istanbul to Karachi and rode the Grand Trunk Road to Calcutta, through eastern China and across Japan, before catching a steamer home to San Francisco. 'Distance actually wheeled, about 13,500 miles,' he recorded.

Crossing the USA in order to, as he said, 'deliver the message',

Stevens followed wagon-roads, railroad ways, canal towpaths and the few public roads that existed. West of the Mississippi River, there were none. For at least a third of the distance, over mountains and deserts, Stevens dragged, shoved, carried and pushed his 75 lb high-wheeler. He was shot at by cowpokes, chased by coyotes and memorably, to avoid being hit by a train, he hung off a railroad bridge above a ravine by one hand, holding

his bicycle in the other.

The drawback of the high-wheeler was the inherent danger of riding one. The saddle was precariously high over the front wheel; the machine pitched forward on encountering the smallest road obstacle, ditching the rider on his head; there were no brakes worth speaking of. Accidents were so common that a new vocabulary was invented to describe them. Riders who went plunging over the front of their bicycles at speed 'took a header', received an 'imperial crowner' or 'came a cropper'. The machines were nicknamed 'widow-makers'. Women didn't ride high-wheelers; nor did boys, nor older men, nor the shortest, or unathletic young men. The machine was a long way from being 'a people's nag', the form of popular, utilitarian transport that society increasingly craved.

In the end, the safety bicycle rapidly made the high-wheeler obsolete. The enduring reputation of the latter is out of proportion to the part it played in the history of the bicycle. This is partly because it has become a symbol of the Victorian era, and partly because of its intriguing shape. It lives on, though, in the calculation of gear sizes (see Appendix), and most significantly in the spare purity of James Starley's tangent-spoked wheel.

When every spoke had been cut to length and rethreaded – by hand in the spoke cutter – then washed, degreased and dried, Gravy applied 'spoke prep' to the threads. He neatly laid out his tools and the components of the wheel on the workbench and pulled up a stool. He hooked a black 'Sapim' apron over his head, sat and checked everything over. He was preparing himself, like a potter sitting down to make a bowl.

'Building a wheel takes you into the zone. It's Zen-like . . . and quite meditative,' Gravy said. 'A result is a wheel as fine as you can build it. If there are ghosts in there, if you're trying to get rid of a micron at the end and then messing it up, that's no good. Like Michelangelo mixing paint, if it's not mixed right the first time, you start over.'

With that Gravy fell silent. He dropped the spokes one by one through the holes in the flanges of the front hub. Periodically, he gathered all the spokes from one side of the hub together and swept them to the side, like someone tying their hair back. When he'd lined up the label on the hub with the label on the rim – a nice touch – he placed the first spoke through the hole on the rim next to the valve and secured it with a blue nipple. All the other nipples would be silver: the blue one was a visual aid, and Gravy's signature. Then he went round the rim once, placing a spoke through every third hole. He flipped the wheel over and laced a second set. Within minutes, the pattern of the wheel began to emerge. He wound the last few nipples on with a homemade tool.

The wheel was laced. If I hadn't seen it, I wouldn't have believed it could be done so quickly. Gravy paused to inspect the pattern: 'When I was wrenching on the road, mechanics from different pro teams would get together and compete. We called it lacing racing.'

He mounted the wheel in his trueing stand, an essential wheel-builder's apparatus that checks the lateral truth of the wheel, and its concentricity or roundness. Working with a spoke key, he made an initial 'pass', tightening each spoke a couple of turns, working back to where he'd started, slowly bringing the spokes uniformly up to tension.

It was a delightful process to watch. Gravy worked slowly and precisely, yet things happened quickly. The parts sat comfortably in his big hands. There was a harmony in the way the spoke wrench moved. It never clattered into the rim or the hub or any of the still slack spokes. It weaved through the air as if it was an appendage to his hand. I realized I was watching a man do what he was a master at – in itself a privilege.

I've seen skilful bike mechanics work their magic and I had anticipated the visual pleasure. I hadn't expected the wheel-building process to be an aural feast too. The metallic brush of the spokes being gathered in hand, the ting of a spoke as the elbow dropped into the flange, the scuffle of the nipples moving on the workbench, the whirr of the wrench fastening the nipples, the swish of the loosely suspended hub flopping about. Ping, ding, tinkle, chink, clink, jangle – as Gravy worked in silence the room was humming with the century-old melody of a bicycle wheel being made. And this was really the opening *allegro* of the symphony. As the spokes began to come up to tension, they clanged and chimed, changing tone with every 'pass' Gravy made round the wheel.

'Sometimes I think I could do it with a blindfold on,' Gravy said, standing for a moment and straightening his back. I could believe this. I'd read about A. G. Duckett & Son, a family run bike shop in East London. It was famous in the 1950s – an era when most bike shops built hoops for their customers – for the quality of its wheels. Despite failing eyesight, damaged during World War II, Albert Duckett used to finish the wheels himself, just by feel and sound.

Gravy can build 100 wheels a week at full steam. I've built one. I was in Piedmont in the Italian Alps. Flying down a mountain road on a bike loaded with panniers, the sidewall on my rear wheel rim came apart. It was late on a Saturday afternoon when I burst through the door of a bike shop in Aosta. The old man who built wheels didn't work on Saturdays. The shop was closed on Sunday, 'naturale'. One of the three young mechanics might have had a go, but Saturday night was looming. I couldn't be sure if it was the taste of cold beer, the whiff of their Mama's ravioli or the touch of a girl's skin that they ached for, but they certainly weren't going to work overtime building me a new hoop.

They did, at least, sell me a new rim at a discount. I sat down on a bench in a square beneath the Roman walls of the town and set to work. I had a set of notes I'd written two years earlier, in Penang, Malaysia. There, too, my rear wheel had failed. I'd written the notes watching Abar, an aged Cantonese-Malayan with mahogany-brown skin cured like leather, build me a wheel. Using pidgin English, Bahasa Malaysian, Cantonese, sign language and drawings, Abar had managed to convey the rudimentary techniques of wheel-building. In the evening, beneath the stucco arch of his bike shop, we ate satay kebabs, coconut-milk rice and mangosteens from the passing hawkers' trolleys. As I rose to leave, Abar tapped the pocket of my shorts where the notes were neatly folded. There was a sense he was passing on a charm.

Sitting on the bench in Aosta, it felt like a curse. I just couldn't get the spokes to lace up correctly. Twice, I laced almost the whole wheel and had to undo it again. As the light began to fade,

I tried a third time. It worked. Each spoke found its true hole. The three-cross pattern was uniform. I trued the wheel laterally as well as I could, using the brake blocks as a makeshift trueing stand. It was the work of an amateur, but I was euphoric. I strapped the panniers back on the bike and set off up the Aosta valley towards the Grand Saint Bernard Pass. On the 25 mile descent to Martigny in Switzerland the next day, the wheel held up. Though it needed almost daily attention, it got me home.

I've still got Abar's notes. I found them recently, neatly folded in the back of my battered 1994 edition of *Richards' Bicycle Repair Manual*. The ink on the verso has soaked through and there are blotches of what could be satay kebabs, but the instructions are legible: (1) Cassette side up, feed 'in bound' spokes in alternate holes . . . (2) Turn hub over. Draw perpendicular line down from spoke nearest valve (get spoke straight); find hole of flange <u>nearest</u> the line of that spoke; take <u>hole on right hand</u> of that and place spoke in. It then goes through on rim, one to right of hole where spoke on other side goes . . .' Re-reading it, I thought it might be code. It was impenetrable. That I used these notes to build a wheel, my first and last, on a bench in a park in Aosta as the aged townsfolk gathered like bluebottles for *passeggiata*, is no less of a wonder to me now than the bicycle wheel itself.

With every spoke uniformly threaded, Gravy put a drop of oil on each nipple – 'to lube the threads, so they won't get damaged when tightening'. Then he stood again to squeeze each pair of spokes in his hands, correcting the spoke line, or 'setting them in' as he called it, 'and looking for flappers'.

For wheels made by machines in a factory, this part of the process is done with a big metal bar, Gravy explained. The potential to over-stress parts of the wheels is huge. It's why factory wheels don't have a long warranty. Gravy's wheels, on the other hand, are guaranteed for life – 'your life, my life or the life of the rim,' he said.

With a tool he's had for twenty-five years, Gravy checked the 'dish', to ensure the rim was centred in the hub, as the front wheel should be. It wasn't. With a few adroit turns of the wrench, he adjusted it. Too much. He adjusted it back, fractionally. The wheel was now ready to be fine-tuned and tensioned.

Gravy started again, at the blue nipple, and tightened every spoke a half turn. As the wheel spun slowly, the trueing stand indicated where the wheel was laterally untrue – the wobbles in the rim walls made a brief scraping noise, like the distant sound of a spade dragging on concrete, as they passed the guides on the apparatus. When Gravy had located the blemish, he worked the relevant spokes: a wobble on the right rim wall, he tightened spokes on the left, and loosened on the right, and vice versa, to make it laterally true. Then he moved on to the next scraping noise, working his way round.

I've trued hundreds of my own wheels, but standing over Gravy's shoulder and seeing the rim change shape and hearing the scrapes fade away with the turn of the spoke key, I had a sense of the wheel being a dynamic and integral structure. A mechanical marvel, yes; simple and beautiful, yes; but somehow alive too. Gravy spun the wheel and stepped back. Light bounced off the stainless steel spokes in a mesmerizing display. For a moment, I was surprised at the dazzling richness of such a practical object. I thought of Marcel Duchamp: he mounted a bicycle wheel upside down on a stool in 1913, spinning it occasionally, and redefined Minimalism. 'I enjoyed looking at it,' Duchamp said. 'Just as I enjoy looking at the flames dancing in the fireplace.'

Gravy went round again – one-quarter turns – and again – one-eighth turns – and again – 'a tiny nudge' – and again – 'to relieve the stress in the spokes.' What could easily be the title of a Fairfax therapy class is actually another important part of the custom wheel-building process. Pairs of parallel spokes are squeezed at midspan on both sides of the wheel, all the way round. It corrects the spoke line at a microscopic level, to make sure they're pulling dead straight, and sets the spoke elbows into the flange. Care must be taken not to overdo it. In a factory, a machine does it. Gravy does it by hand with an aged tool made for him out of an axle, by Tom Ritchey.

With a spoke tension meter in hand, Gravy began the final finessing. James Starley would have given his eye-teeth for one of these tools. It measures the bend in millimetres between three points on a spoke and gives a figure in Newtons for the tension of that spoke. It's a way of ensuring, with remarkable accuracy, that each spoke is at the optimum tension. It's a long way from the coarse lever Starley used to tension the wheels on the first Ariel bicycles.

'The more you ride your bike, the more you want nice wheels,' Gravy said softly. 'Taken care of properly, overhauled from time to time and not left out to rust, a wheel can last you decades . . . and give you all sorts of fun rides.'

Gravy raised his wrench to the wheel less and less, and then not at all. It spun in silence. He stood up, stepped back and put his arm around my shoulder.

'Well, my friend. It's true.'

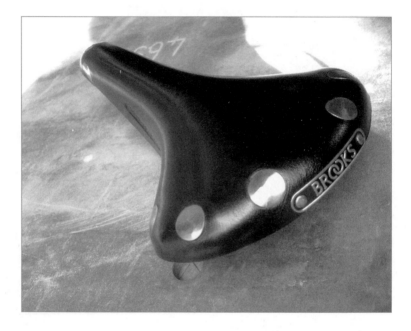

5. On the Rivet

The Saddle

Truth hurts. Maybe not as much as jumping on a bicycle
with a seat missing, but it hurts.

(Leslie Nielsen, *Naked Gun 2½*)

There are three contact points between rider and bicycle: hands/
handlebar, feet/pedals and backside/saddle. Their order of impor-
tance depends largely on how dedicated a cyclist you are. Ride
100 miles with an avid cyclist and he may complain a little about
pain in his wrists or ankles; ride 10 miles with a novice and he
will bellyache about his backside until he's had three pints and a
bag of pork rinds. Nothing kills the joy of a bicycle ride like
saddle-sore. It's the most common complaint in cycling and
there's a good case for the inclusion in the English language of
an intransitive verb that describes the precise condition: to buttache – *v.i.* (slang) to complain whiningly about saddle-sore from
riding a bicycle.

A universal truth of bicycling is this – pain is inevitable,
suffering is optional. Pro cyclists hurt badly too. They just don't
buttache about it. In *The Sun Also Rises* by Ernest Hemingway – a
keen cyclist who rode round Europe with F. Scott Fitzgerald –
the protagonist Jake Barnes encounters a group of professional
racing cyclists at dinner in a Spanish hotel during a stage-race:

The bicycle-riders drank much wine, and were burned and browned by the sun . . . The man who had a matter of two-minutes lead in the race had an attack of boils, which were very painful. He sat on the small of his back . . . The other riders joked with him about his boils. He tapped on the table with his fork. 'Listen,' he said, 'tomorrow my nose is so tight on the handlebars that the only thing touches those boils is a lovely breeze.'

The damage a saddle can do to the human body is extraordinary. I've never had boils on my backside, but friction with a piece of leather has, in the past, caused cuts, lacerations, lesions, abrasions and contusions. I've rubbed my thighs raw like sashimi. The term 'saddle-sore' doesn't come close to expressing the pain. 'Saddle trauma' is nearer the mark.

Comfort is the only requirement of a bicycle saddle. The basic ergonomic principles behind it are simple. The front end or nose of a saddle is narrow, to prevent (or at least limit) chafing of the inner thigh. The rear is wide enough to support the rider's pelvic girdle: or, to be anatomically exact, to support the 'ischial tuberosities' or 'sit bones'. This is the part of your backside that bears your weight when you sit. Women have sit bones half an inch or so farther apart than men (it's to do with giving birth), and so benefit from saddles a little wider at the rear.

The shape of a saddle becomes critical when cycling over long distances, where the rider applies great force and pedals fast, as pros do. In the days of leather saddles, which shape to fit through use, pro cyclists took comfy saddles with them when they changed teams. Tommy Simpson, the flawed British cycling hero who was more famous in death than life, used to make his own saddles. Horst Schütz, a German pro in the 1980s, had saddles specially made for him: hollows and bumps were carved into the compressed foam to replicate the anomalies of his bony behind.

Simpson and Schütz were both noted track racers who took part in many modern 'six-day races' – a form of competitive cycle racing that perhaps provides the ultimate test of the backside/saddle interface. In the early days, races literally went on for six days and nights, non-stop. Individuals cycled as many laps of an indoor cycle track as they could in the time. The first competitive six-day race was held in the Islington Agricultural Hall, London, in 1878. Riders, on high-wheeler bicycles, rode round and round until they dropped, slept briefly, rose, and rode round and round again – for six days straight. There was no racing on the Sabbath. Phew! As sport, it would not meet with the customs of our times.

Victorian society, however, took delight in observing the blind animal endurance of poorly paid athletes. Thousands filled the Hall each day to watch the riders pile on the laps. The winner, the *Islington Gazette* reported, was Bill Cann of Sheffield. He rode 1,756 km (1,060 miles) on a bicycle with a wooden saddle. What the *Gazette* did not report was that his buttaching could be heard in Lincolnshire.

The following year, the same event was dubbed the 'Long Distance Championship of the World'. As a purely commercial enterprise, it was outside the remit of the newly founded, self-styled governing bodies of cycling – the Bicycle Union and the British Touring Club (later the Cyclists' Touring Club). Typical of the priggishness that dominated this new age of athleticism in Britain, the two organizations barred from membership anyone who had ever won prize money or been paid to compete. Cycling was at the forefront of the rationalization of sport then emanating from the universities and public schools, and central to one of the period's big social questions: the 'Gentlemen vs. Players' debate – should people be paid for playing sport? Football, cricket and rugby were, roughly simultaneously, going through the same growing pains.

Few 'Gentlemen' fancied the indignity of a six-day race, of course. George Waller, a professional cyclist and general Newcastle brick, won the 1879 event, and 100 guineas. He averaged well over 322 km (200 miles) a day and had to be carried from his saddle at the finish. After a brief business excursion with a travelling cyclists' circus, he retired as a pro and went back to work as a builder.

M. CHARLES TERRONT
Vainqueur de la course nationale de Paris à Brest
organisée par le « Petit Journal »

Waller's main rival in 1879 was Frenchman, Charles Terront. Also working class, he prospered, unlike Waller, which says much about social mobility in the two countries. Terront became France's first sports star (there's a street named after him in Nantes), with riches, a memoir published during his lifetime, many female admirers and a reserved seat at the Opéra in Paris. His success made him an icon for successive generations of working-class Frenchmen who sought the mansion on the hill through cycle racing. Terront advanced from six-day racing to other track disciplines and then, most famously, to road racing. In 1891, after 71 hours and 22 minutes of continuous, sleepless racing, Terront rode down the Champs-Elysées alone. He'd won the first Paris–Brest–Paris race, the oldest extant 'Classic' cycle race and inspiration for the

Tour de France (which began in 1903, as a six-day race on the *road* instead of the track). At 745 miles, Paris–Brest–Paris was another mean test of a bicycle saddle. At least they were by then made not of wood but of leather.

Six-day races or 'Sixes' reached New York in the early 1890s, signalling the beginning of the cycling frenzy that swept across America. From the mid-1890s to the end of the 1920s, every major US city had a velodrome. Along with baseball, track racing was the most popular spectator sport. The annual races at Madison Square Garden were the largest and most spectacular sporting events of the era, dubbed the 'Super Bowl of Sixes'. (Still a popular type of track race today, 'the Madison' is named after the venue.) The carnival-like atmosphere and the opportunity to socialize and bet attracted an extraordinary cross-section of Manhattan society. Captains of industry and politicians mixed with movie stars and gangsters, all watched over by bookies and eagle-eyed promoters in white suits and blue spats.

The 300 or so US manufacturers of bicycles vied to sponsor the leanest, fastest, most handsome cyclists. Their fortunes rose and fell with them. Cyclists were the highest earners in sport: in fact, modern professional sports marketing effectively began with them. For a brief period, before motorcycles and automobiles, men on bicycles whirling round banked cycling tracks made of Siberian pine were the fastest things on the planet. And speed was the currency of the moment. Professional cyclists found themselves the gods of sport. At the Garden, they were all-powerful.

Add to the sponsorship battles America's favourite pastime, gambling, and the scene was set to push the riders to their limits. There were numerous accidents, as riders fell unconscious and lurched across the track. Drugs were taken, merely to keep the riders awake. Occasionally they rode themselves to death. The crowds revelled 'in a kind of agony and suffering that perhaps was available only on the battlefield,' Todd Balf wrote in his biography of Major Taylor. Taylor launched his racing career at a six-day race at Madison Square Garden in 1896, the year the first six-day race for women was held. During the event Taylor collapsed and feared he might die. However, he went on to become a great track sprinter, a sporting icon and America's first black celebrity, at a time when such a thing was deemed improper.

In 1897, Charlie Miller rode 3,369 km (2,093 miles) in a Six at the Garden, winning the cash prize of $3,550 and a kiss from a music hall beauty. He told reporters he'd eaten three pounds of boiled rice and a pound of oatmeal and drunk several gallons of coffee and twenty quarts of milk. In six days, he pedalled for all but a total of ten hours.

In response to protests, a New York State law was introduced in 1898 prohibiting cyclists from riding more than twelve hours a day: two-man teams were introduced. Speeds rose and distances grew. Sponsorship from manufacturers continued to pour in. The top riders, the 'Stars of the Saucer', earned in six days what their fathers had earned in six years. The great Australian cyclist Alf Goullet and his partner rode a staggering 4,442 km (2,759 miles) in the six-day event at Madison Square Garden in 1914. That's near enough the width of the USA, from 'sea to shining sea'. It's 600 miles (966 km) further than the modern Tour de France, which takes three weeks. It remains the record today. Goullet wrote after the event, 'My knees were sore, I was suffering from stomach trouble, my hands were so numb I couldn't open them wide enough to button my collar for a month, and my eyes were so irritated I couldn't, for a long time, stand smoke in a room.' Note no buttaching. Goullet won fifteen six-day races including eight at Madison Square Garden. He lived to be 103.

The list of historical sporting events that I wish I had attended is long. Along with the bicycle, history and sport are my passions. Give me the keys to Doctor Who's TARDIS and I'd take in Iffley Road athletics track in 1954 to watch Roger Bannister break the four-minute barrier for the mile. Next I'd go to Cardiff Arms Park for the Barbarians v. New Zealand in 1973. Then to West London in December 1810 to catch perhaps the greatest prizefight ever – Cribb v. Molyneaux. After that, one of the epic, annual six-day events at the Garden in either the mid-1890s or the early 1920s would be my next stop.

By the 1920s, with Prohibition in force, the glamorous *demimonde* of the Jazz Age mingled with celebrities such as Bing Crosby at the Garden. Over 125,000 attended the 1922 event. 'Coal-heavers, mechanics, cab drivers and clerks' caroused with 'white shirt-fronts and low-cut gowns,' a journalist reported. The 'Races to Nowhere' made headline news. Damon Runyon reported on Sixes for the *New York Times* and Ring Lardner wove them into the temper of the times via his sporting columns. The visceral intensity attracted Hemingway. He attended many six-day races in Paris in the 1920s, and edited the proof of *A Farewell to Arms* in a box at the Vélodrome d'Hiver in 1929:

'I have started many stories about bicycle racing but have never written one that is as good as the races are,' he wrote in *A Moveable Feast*.

In *The Great Bicycle Expedition*, the author William Anderson met a 70-year-old former six-day racer, who recalled: 'Six days of chafing your inner thighs on a pie-shaped piece of leather. You'd be amazed at the things bike riders have used to reduce the friction. I personally have tried axle grease, Vaseline, coconut oil, you name it. Fellow I knew even tried a preliminary heat with his shorts stuffed with Jell-o . . . Ah, those were the days.'

Sixes in America faded in popularity during the Great Depression. Automobile-mania and televised sport had killed them off completely by the 1940s. By the time Horst Schütz was creating his undulating saddles in the 1980s, the vestiges of the six-day racing calendar were back in Europe. Today, the races are nothing like the extreme endurance events loved by the Victorians. Nevertheless, in Amsterdam, Berlin, Bremen and Stuttgart, and at the legendary 'Six-Days of Ghent', pro cyclists do still put their rears where it hurts, and put their saddles to the ultimate test.

I've tried many saddles. None have been what I'd call comfortable in the same way as a pair of old slippers. I've noticed, though, that I do become inured to the pain of different saddles at different speeds. This suggests some saddles are better, or at least suit me better, than others. It does not suggest, as one of the characters asserts in *Three Men on the Bummel* by Jerome K. Jerome, 'that the right saddle is to be found'. Jerome is rightly sceptical:

I said: 'You give up that idea; this is an imperfect world of joy and sorrow mingled. There may be a better land where bicycle saddles are made out of rainbow, stuffed with cloud; in this world the simplest thing is to get used to something hard. There was the saddle you bought in Birmingham; it was divided in the middle and looked like a pair of kidneys.'

[Harris] said: 'You mean that one constructed on anatomical principles?'

'Very likely,' I replied. 'The box you bought it in had a picture on the cover, representing a sitting skeleton . . . I only know that I tried it myself, and that to a man who wore flesh it was agony. Every time you went over a stone or a rut it nipped you; it was like riding on an irritable lobster.'

Three Men on the Bummel, about a cycling tour through the Black Forest, was first published in 1900. Jerome was a gimlet-eyed social observer and witness to the unseemly rush to make a fortune from bicycles during the 1890s. Once pedals, a chain drive, brakes and pneumatic tyres had been added to the diamond-shaped frame, the inventors' attentions turned, finally, to making the saddle comfortable.

John Kemp Starley famously sat down hard on a heap of wet sand, pointed to the imprint of his buttocks and exclaimed to his employees, 'Make that!' 'New' saddles were advertised almost continuously in the 1890s. The ads often proclaimed 'ground-breaking' medical evidence showing just how detrimental the 'old' style of saddle was. Chaps like Harris couldn't help themselves as Jerome noted: 'Can you think of any saddle ever advertised that you have *not* tried?'

One earlier, novel attempt to remove the threat of male impotence caused by cycling on cobblestone roads came from the Boston Athletic Club. A group of 'bike jockeys', as cyclists were known in America during the 1870s, sought an undergarment that supported and protected the groin while in the saddle, without attracting accusations of corrupting public morals. At their bidding, Charles Bennett of the Chicago sporting goods company

Sharp & Smith invented the 'Bike Jockey Strap', or jockstrap.

Saddles for women were a particular concern to the conservative elements of Victorian society. That bike riding might be sexually stimulating to women was a real worry. Of course, the threat of tens of thousands of permanently aroused nymphomaniacs cruising around the countryside on bicycles never materialized. The saddle manufacturers had a field day even so. In 1895, the first 'Hygienic' saddle was produced. Marketed as 'anatomically perfect', the saddle was divided in two, so the rider's weight rested on his or her ischial tuberosities solely. It is probably the very design that Jerome K. Jerome likened to 'riding on an irritable lobster'.

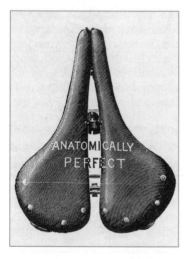

Anatomical saddles are still patented and manufactured today. In fact, each generation since the Victorians has produced someone who thinks he's cracked the problem with some freakish adaptation of the saddle. And, like Harris, we keep on buying them. I've seen 'wonder saddles' shaped like old-style tractor seats (two cheek scoops and no pommel), or like the snout of a great anteater, a new moon, the seat of a shooting stick, a circle of black pudding, a manta ray, oversized tuning forks set in an oven glove, and the upper section of a potty. In my opinion, they're all made by quacks. The websites selling them invariably claim to redefine comfort, and headline with the familiar question: 'Impotence: are you at risk?'

The more enlightened version of a woman-specific saddle has a groove cut out along the centre, and a slightly shortened nose.

Manufacturers started producing these 'cutaway' saddles a century ago and they remain popular. It's a simple modification to the standard saddle design with sound anatomical and medical reasoning behind it: taking a chunk out of the middle of a saddle reduces pressure on some highly sensitive parts of the body.

The most uncomfortable saddle I've ever ridden was the largest. It was on my first real bike, a Raleigh Tomahawk. It was black and spongy, with a backrest. It taught me the first rule of the bicycle saddle at an early age: less is more. I learnt rule two when, aged 12, I got my first drop handlebar bike: the width of the saddle depends on the position of the upper body on the bicycle. When you're crouched over the bike with your hands in the 'Ds' of the handlebars and your spine curved, a narrow saddle is more functional. Sitting upright on a commuter bike, a wider saddle is preferable.

On my first mountain bike adventure to China and Pakistan, I bought a saddle cover in the bazaar in the city of Urumqi. It consisted of two inches of foam covered in purple velvet. Braids and sequins adorned the sides. It looked like a stray shoulder pad from a jacket Huggy Bear might have worn, working undercover at a pimp convention. It had no place on a mountain bike. Halfway along the Karakoram Highway between Kashgar and Gilgit, I was walking like John Wayne. Rule three: never adorn a saddle with *anything*. Excessive sponginess or layers of extra padding may initially seem more comfortable, but they make for more lateral movement, inefficient pedalling and, ultimately, suffering. I got away with it relatively lightly that time. My friend Bill bought the same saddle cover in green velvet. Deep in the Hindu Kush, he got haemorrhoids.

Different saddles adorn my current fleet of bikes. On my old Schwinn mountain bike, I have a Selle San Marco 'Rolls'. San Marco has been making saddles in northern Italy since 1935. The

Rolls model is something of a classic. The saddle is made of high-density foam and covered with leather. It's really a saddle for a high-performance racing bike – Bernard Hinault and Greg LeMond both won Tours de France in the 1980s on Rolls – but it looks grand on my old warhorse. However, if I don't ride this bike for a few months, the Rolls feels like a piece of granite. My newer mountain bike has a proprietary saddle: it's slim and comfortable but it's covered in vinyl and looks cheap. Both my racing bikes have saddles made by Selle Italia – in the business since 1897, one of the venerated marques of Italian bicycle componentry and manufacturer of the first genuinely minimalist saddle, in the 1980s. The old aluminium racer has a 'cutaway' saddle that is fraying and curling at the edges. The newer carbon bike has an über-sleek, black convex saddle with a chunk missing out of the rear – the result of a high-speed encounter with Joe Tarmac. On my aged commuter bike, there is a nondescript, large foam saddle. I can't remember where it came from. It's easily the least comfortable.

Save for the latter, these saddles are all high quality and slightly different. Yet it seems that no matter which bike I jump on, some days my backside hurts and some days it doesn't.

There is one saddle I haven't mentioned: the saddle on which I rode round the world. I remember the conversation with the assistant in the workshop where the frame was to be built. After the fitting process, we were going through the checklist of components that would be assembled on my bike. The assistant knew well what I needed but he was polite enough to humour me. He initiated a short debate about the best rims, spokes, racks, handlebars, brakes and so on, before leading me to his pre-formed conclusion. When it came to the saddle, though, there was no such courtesy. Without looking up from the page, he wrote down 'B 17'.

'What's a B 17?' I asked. 'It sounds like a cocktail.' He pointed to the saddle on the bike behind me.

'That's what my Granddad rode on,' I said.

'Precisely.'

Brooks make B 17 saddles. John Boultbee Brooks founded the company in Birmingham in 1866, to make horse harnesses and other leather goods. Twelve years later, so the story goes, the horse Brooks rode to work went off to the great steeplechase in the sky. Unable to afford a new horse, Brooks borrowed a bicycle to commute. Like many gentlemen of his age, he presumably found this iron horse something of a revelation, not least because he didn't have to feed it a bucket of oats each day. He certainly found the wooden saddle a revelation: it was so uncomfortable Brooks swore he'd do something about it.

In October 1882, he applied for his first saddle patent. It read: 'My invention has for its object the construction of saddles for Bicycles and Tricycles so that they shall be more comfortable and easy especially when in continual use.' The company has been devoted to relieving the problems of cyclists' posteriors ever since. Mr Brooks, on behalf of bike riders the world over, and through the ages, I salute you, you beautiful man.

Brooks introduced the B 17 in 1896. It's been in continuous production ever since. I suspect this makes it the oldest extant component model in the history of the bicycle. Such longevity is the result of several things: a new B 17 is an object of beauty; the succinct name is memorable in many languages; the simple design has hardly changed; and traditional manufacturing techniques have been passed down from generation to generation of craftsmen who all honour the company's heritage. Above all, though, the saddles are comfortable and they are built to last.

During the twentieth century Brooks diversified into saddlebags, toolbags, panniers, bicycle-mounted cigar trays (what gentleman would ride without one?) and even furniture. The company changed hands a couple of times – it was briefly part of Raleigh – but Brooks never stopped making B 17s to the most exacting standards. For almost fifty years, until the 1970s, the B 17 was the saddle of choice for the majority of professional racers including those from France, Italy and the Netherlands, who were presumably under pressure to ride on saddles made in their home countries. The vast majority of serious cyclists followed the pros' lead.

Moulded plastic, vinyl, titanium, Kevlar, spray adhesives and gel (a type of durable, non-absorbent foam) were introduced to saddles from the mid-1970s onwards. It was a fundamental change. Saddles became lighter and cheaper to make. Leather faded from fashion. When my round-the-world bike was being built in 1995, the B 17 was serving only a niche market – long-distance tourers. Of these, there were two types: young men and women setting off to cross continents, and the dying breed of British cyclists setting off to a youth hostel with a neatly folded map and a thermos of soup. In 1995, Brooks saddles were not the height of cool (though they are again now: sales have trebled in seven years since 2002).

The frame-builder's assistant inked 'B 17' on to my order form without a moment's hesitation, as the manager of the Brazilian football team at the 1970 World Cup Finals would have inked in 'Pelé' at number 10. That saddle lasted me for 25,000 miles. I'm not saying it didn't cause any pain – pain is inevitable, remember – but I didn't suffer.

By the time I got back to the UK, I'd all but pounded the poor saddle to death with my buttocks. The leather had slipped away from the rivets at the rear, and torn at the side. The rails – the steel under-carriage that connects the saddle to the seat post – had a small crack. But my B 17 saw me home.

Spending so much time on one saddle does carry a risk, if you believe Sergeant Pluck in Flann O'Brien's bizarre, satirical tale of a tender but unrequited love affair between a man and a bicycle, *The Third Policeman*. Pluck's 'Atomic Theory' says prolonged contact with a bicycle saddle can result in 'molecular exchange':

The gross and net result of it is that people who spend most of their natural lives riding iron bicycles over rocky roadsteads of this parish get their personalities mixed up with the personalities of their bicycles as a result of the interchanging of the atoms of each of them and you would be surprised at the number of people in these parts who are nearly half people and half bicycle.

The Brooks factory is down a side street in Smethwick, near the Birmingham Canal Navigations. Smethwick was a rural hamlet before the industrial revolution turned it into a nineteenth-century boomtown and global centre of metalworking expertise. Today, Brooks is the only bicycle-related manufacturing business left, not just in Smethwick but in the whole of the greater Birmingham area. They make saddles and a small range of leather bicycle accessories.

The Brooks factory has been on the same site in Downing Street since 1950, when the company made cables, handlebars, brakes and, briefly, complete bicycles. It requires a great leap of imagination to picture Birmingham then. Known as the 'City of a thousand trades', nearly every non-domestic building would have been a factory or workshop making nails, guns, tools,

cutlery, bedsteads, castings, toys, locks and bicycle parts. The
city's growth and prosperity depended upon metalworking industries, and at the heart of this was the bicycle.

With Coventry to the south-east and Nottingham to the
north-east, Birmingham made up a triangle that contained the
largest concentration of bicycle and bicycle component manufacturers on the planet. It was home to Hercules, the world's
largest bicycle manufacturer in the 1930s, plus hundreds of
businesses that made everything from bearings to steel tubes. My
Dad grew up between Birmingham and Coventry. One of his
earliest memories is watching the night sky flame orange as the
bicycle factories and car plants in Coventry burned, during the
Blitz. When I told him I was writing a book about the bike, he
was delighted. His generation of Midlanders still have a sense of
ownership of the bicycle.

Steven Green, the office manager or 'gaffer' to his thirty
employees, met me at the factory door. 'Welcome to Brooks,' he
said loudly over the noise of the 'press shop'. Blanking, bending
and riveting machines were hammering, shaping, coiling and
cutting steel. The sound-track of the factory – once the sound-
track of the whole City – can hardly have changed in a century,
I suggested.

'That's right,' Steven said with a twinkling eye. 'Some of the
employees have been here almost as long too. Meet Bob.'

Bob, an avuncular figure with kind eyes and worn hands,
was operating a blanking machine making coil springs for the
suspension in Brooks' legendary range of heavy-duty saddles. He
smiled broadly. 'Aye, I've been working here for fifty years. It's
just with a gaffer like him it feels longer. Now, the only thing
here even older than me is this here machine. It's from the 1940s.
Fortunately we can still get spare parts for it. I wish I could say
the same for me.'

Next I met Keith. He'd worked at Brooks for forty years. Then Stephen – over thirty years; Alan – nineteen years; and Beverley – 'not telling'.

'We're really like a family, a second family,' Steven said, straightening his tie again. Clearly he took pride in this. 'Everyone gets on with everyone else. We have a good social life. There's a lot of training involved. And there's so much pride taken in what we do that people want to stay. Customers bring in saddles that are thirty or forty years old, for an overhaul. That's very nice.'

Putting a hand on my shoulder as we walked across the press shop to the leather-working room, Bob said, 'Think of a Brooks saddle like a pair of leather shoes. They may be uncomfortable when you first put them on. They'll pinch a bit here and nip a bit there. But after a while they fit beautifully and they'll be the most comfortable shoes you have for twenty years. I always say bike riders use plastic saddles; cyclists use leather.'

New Brooks saddles are notoriously hard compared to modern gel-padded saddles. Like Bob's leather shoes or a baseball glove, they need 'breaking in'. Aficionados clash on how best to do this. Some hurry the process by applying lanoline leather dressing. Brooks suggest their own 'Proofide' ointment. In the end, to break in a Brooks saddle, you have to ride it.

After 1,000 miles there will be shallow indentations where your sit bones are and the leather will have moulded to fit your backside. My B 17 took a little longer. The first leg of my round-the-world journey was from New York to San Francisco. I recall thinking the saddle was finally comfortable somewhere in South Dakota. Thereafter, I had no problems. If you take the trouble to keep the leather taut using the tensioning bolt (a defining feature of Brooks saddles), the saddle will only continue getting more comfortable.

You have then a product that improves with use. This is an

anomaly. We live in a dystopian age when almost everything we buy begins to deteriorate the moment it comes out of the box. *Tout passe, tout casse, tout lasse* as the French say – everything changes, everything breaks, everything wears out. Obsolescence is ubiquitous. We've come to accept it as the norm. Buy it, use it, bury it in the ground. A Brooks saddle, with its legendary lifespan, could be one of the first products of a utopian economy: the sort of economy dissident intellectuals were dreaming up in the 1970s, wherein goods are expensive, built to last and repairable. Ideally the people who made them would be well paid and share in the wealth.

It was difficult to see Steven and Bob as the advance guard of the greatest economical (and ecological) transition the world has known since the beginning of the industrial revolution. And to be perfectly honest, when I suggested it to them, they didn't know what I was talking about.

The leather for the saddles comes from British and Irish cattle, via a tannery in Belgium. It has to be 5.5–6 mm thick, 'for proper support, and to last. Only the section of the hide from the shoulder blade to the butt is thick enough,' Steven explained, handing me a black sheet of it. I watched the leather being cut into saddle shapes, like pastry cases. Any blemished sections were discarded. It was then soaked in tepid water and pressed on to a brass saddle mould, before being dried and shaped again. Beverley smoothed the edges of the leather on a huge belt sander. The trademark was branded on with a heating element. The company badge was fixed to the rear and the leather was hung on a rack with hundreds of other part-prepared saddles and run on a trolley to the assembly stations.

The whole process of making a saddle takes three days. Each job requires a high level of hand–eye co-ordination, manual dexterity and concentration. 'Experience and a good eye are important,' Steven said. 'You'd have a good chance of losing a hand if you had a go at any of these jobs.' I did look to see if anyone was short a finger or two, but no. Even Sonia, who was punching rivets through leather to mount it on the metal cantle plates, with only experience and a good eye to guide her, had the full complement.

'On the rivet' is an old cycling expression. It dates from the era when all saddles were made of leather and secured to the frame with metal rivets. It describes a rider scrunched tight and low on his bike, hands clamped to the drops and backside perched precariously on the nose of the saddle, trying to lever maximum power into the machine with every pedal stroke, going at it for all he's worth. 'On the gel' somehow doesn't convey the same intensity.

The models with large brass rivets are hammered and chamfered by hand – jobs no machine can do – to finish them off. Chamfering is a medieval carpentry term for fluting the edge of something. At Brooks, Eric shaves the edge of the leather away with a razor-sharp tool in a continuous motion. A momentary loss of concentration causing a slip of the tool and that saddle is heading for the bin. The 'Team Professional' model is chamfered. When pro cyclists rode Brooks saddles, they used to complain that the edge of the saddle rubbed their thighs. Today, the process is more for decoration but it illustrates better than anything else the care and the precision of the handwork that goes into every saddle. It reveals why Brooks has become a byword for good craftsmanship.

'We make over forty models. Each one requires different workmanship. And if you're chamfering or even riveting, you have to get a feel for each batch of leather as they're all different,' Steven said. We walked back across the factory to the end of the production line where the saddles were being inspected one last time, polished and boxed.

'Now,' he said. 'You've seen the manufacturing process from start to finish. I presume it's a B 17 you want to buy. What colour?'

'Actually, I'm going for a Team Professional instead. I've fallen for the hand-hammered copper rivets and the chamfering. I'd like a black one with a chrome frame.' The Team Professional was introduced in 1963. At 46 years old, it's the whippersnapper in the Brooks range. Based on the B 17, it is constructed from a single piece of leather shaped over a steel frame of two rails and the curved cantle plate. The tensioning bolt is fixed underneath the nose and the leather is secured with copper rivets front and rear. 'Team Professional' is branded on both sides and a 'Brooks' plate is fixed to the rear. It is simple and beautiful, a blend of strength and grace. I could see the warm approval in Steven's eyes.

'Good choice,' he said. 'It should serve you well for many years to come. And I hope you'll bring it back in twenty-five years for an overhaul. Some of us will no doubt still be working here then.'

Not in Vain the Distance Beckons

A road, a mile of kingdom, I am king
Of banks and stones and every blooming thing.

(Patrick Kavanagh, 'Inniskeen Road: July Evening')

The seasons changed twice between my first visit to Brian Rourke and my return to see the bike being painted and assembled. In that time, I'd considered a hundred colours. Some had been summoned to mind deliberately. Others had dropped in uninvited during my journey to collect the components. The first colour to stick was yellow – a rich Van Gogh yellow, a Mediterranean hue that cycling made its own when the leader of the Tour de France first pulled on *le maillot jaune* in 1919. The colour was chosen to reflect the pages of *L'Auto*, the newspaper that backed the event. Next, I wanted a black bike – it would look suave and ageless, I thought. Then a friend said black carried a psychological burden and would make the bike look heavy. I dabbled with Bianchi-blue or 'celeste', made iconic by Fausto Coppi and said to be the colour of the Queen of Italy's eyes. I toyed with British racing green, until I read it represented greed.

My wife is an artist. She has great taste in colour. When I asked her what she thought of Cappuccino-brown – the colour of self-sacrifice – she said: 'Darling, is choosing a colour for your bike harder than choosing a name for your children?' That wasn't helpful. The Malteser-orange of Eddy Merckx's bikes, seal-grey, pearlescent grey, raspberry, azure, crimson, sapphire, sea-green and myrtle – I mulled over them all until my dreams were filled with flickering colour swatches. I printed dozens of photos of hand-painted bikes and stuck them to the walls of my office. Still, I couldn't choose.

The decision was complicated by having to find a second colour for the contrasting panels on the down tube and the seat tube. I rang Jason Rourke. He would be painting the frame: 'I need guidance,' I said. 'What colours *can* I have?'

'Any colour you can think of, Rob. Any colour you fancy. Basically, any colour at all.'

'Nope, you can't have that colour,' Jason said, putting a paint-pot down, turning to face me, resting his hips against the workbench, crossing his ankles and folding his arms. We were in his paint-shop.

'What do you mean, "No"?' I said.

'Just no. That's it. No.'

'You can't say that. I'm the customer. And you said I can have any colour.'

'Rob, one day you will thank me for this. It may even be today. But there's no way I'm going to paint your bike purple. It's not 1973. We're not going off to see a Slade concert tonight. I promise you, if you had that bike purple, you'd be back here in six months begging me to re-spray it. No.'

Purple had come to me late in the journey. I had an imperial purple in mind: Tyrian purple – the dye first produced by the ancient Phoenicians, the colour of clotted blood.

'You're not Ziggy Stardust,' Jason said. 'You're just Rob Penn. How about Flamboyant Red? That's popular.'

Along with choosing the tubing material, the right geometry, the perfectly sized frame to suit the rider's needs and the components to match it, choosing the colour scheme goes to the heart of why you would want a bespoke bicycle. Not only should the bike feel and handle like it was made for you, it should look like your bike too. Red – one of the periodic favourites of the mass manufacturers – would not do.

'I've just painted a bike I made for Muhammad Ali in Flamboyant Red over silver, with pearl white panels. If it's good enough for Muhammad Ali, it's good enough for you,' Jason said.

'No.'

'Gunmetal grey? That's been in demand in the last few years, with blue or red panels.' Jason continued rummaging among the fifty or so tins of paint on the shelves in front of us. He popped the lids with a screwdriver and pushed the tins along the bench towards me.

'Pink?'

'No.'

'Ferrari blue?'

'Umm . . .'

Pop . . . pop . . . pop. There were three tins of different metallic blues in front of me.

'That one's a Harley-Davidson blue. Quite electric. A bit like sapphire but richer . . . Now this one's a nice colour – a metallic blue with a clear top coat so you can build up the top coat to make it as dark as you want.'

'I like this blue,' I said, pulling one tin to the side. 'What would that go with, for the contrasting panels? Blue and orange?'

Jason's lips tightened. Blue and orange are my favourite colours. In all my efforts to find a unique colour scheme, I'd overlooked them.

'Can we see an orange?' I said.

'Nnnn – all right. We're never gonna agree on this, are we?'

While I flicked through booklets of colour swatches, Jason rooted through another hundred or more tins of paint in the cupboard.

'Californian Gold? Olympic Gold? Candy-apple Red? Here we go, here's an electric orange,' he said, passing a tin over his head. 'That's what Jeremy Clarkson calls ASBO orange. Here's another . . . and another. Let's have a look at these.'

With all the tins of orange and blue in front of me, I finally had a target in sight. For an hour, I deliberated, shuffling the tins around, placing each orange with each blue and trying to imagine them together on a frame. It was difficult. Jason had left me to it. The silence was only broken by the repeated thump of my clenched fist meeting the palm of my other hand. Just when I wondered if I might be getting high on the fumes of the paint, the perfect blue and orange combination hit me.

'OK, I've got it,' I shouted downstairs. Jason came doubling up the steps.

'Quick,' he said. 'Let's get on with it before you change your mind.'

Jason was into his white romper suit and halfway to looking like a Droog before I could say 'Clockwork Orange'. The frame had already been prepped with white paint. The seat and chain stays were wrapped in paper and sealed – they would remain unpainted, giving the frame a classic, Italian look. This was one thing we had agreed on. With the frame hanging from a meat hook, he set to work. The first coat of orange went on the seat tube and the down tube. It looked awful. I whimpered.

'The colour changes with each coat. In fact, you can't really judge until the painting is finished and the bike's been built up. So don't worry . . . yet.'

Another coat went on. The 'oven', a heated panel at the back of the paint shop, ensured each coat was dry in minutes. After the third coat of orange, Jason masked off the panels with tape and paper, and filled the spray canister with blue.

Many frame-builders send their frames out to be painted. I can understand why. It is a specialized job – perhaps as difficult to master as the welding itself. The masking needs deft handwork; knowing when paint is taking and how it changes colour as coats build up requires experience, and getting every coat even is a skill. The paintwork is also the criterion by which many potential customers will judge a hand-built bicycle: few will inspect the tube welds and even fewer will know what they're looking for. Everyone, however, can spot a botched paint job.

Jason worked carefully, making elegant sweeps with the spray gun to ensure the entire frame received each coat smoothly. Between coats three and four, he pulled out a drawer of transfers or 'decals'. I needed to choose them for the down tube and the seat tube: 'ROURKE' in silver over the orange panels, with multi-coloured World Championship bands to edge the panels; the elegant Brian Rourke logo on the head tube and a smaller 'BR' badge on the rear of the seat post – 'so, when you drop somebody, Rob, they know you're riding a Rourki,' Jason said. The final transfer, on the top tube, would be my name: 'Rob Penn', in a simple font, in silver.

'Is it dark enough? Tell me if the blue is dark enough for you. I can easily make it darker if you want, but I think it's building up nicely now,' Jason said, finishing another coat. The power to make a decision had left me. It was dark outside now. I was almost mute with anxiety about whether the blue and orange would go together. Jason put one more coat of blue on. When it was dry, he worked away the tape with a scalpel, and carefully peeled back the paper from the panels.

Blue and orange. It looked fucking fabulous.

If seeing the frame being painted was agony, watching the bike being assembled in Brian Rourke's shop was uninterrupted pleasure. Matt Roberts, the chief mechanic, worked with the precision and dexterity of a watchmaker. First, inner tubes and the tyres were attached to the wheels, taking care to ensure the writing on the tyre aligned with the valve hole. Next, with the bare frame mounted on a workstand, the head tube was prepared. The bearing cups of the headset were pressed in and the steering system – forks, stem and handlebar – came together.

I had brought all the components to the shop in a large cardboard box. Each time Matt bent down and pulled something out, a memory came dashing back – Gravy's vast hands, Antonio Colombo's suit, the twinkle in Steven Green's eye. It was like an evocative lucky dip, a box of happy remembrances.

The bottom bracket, chainset and cassette were next. Matt plucked tools from the arsenal on the wall behind him, often reaching for them without looking. The front and rear derailleurs were bolted on, then the chain. Manufactured to standard size, Matt shortened it to the correct length for my bike with a chain tool, by eye. Then he drove the connecting rivet into place: the drivetrain was complete.

The wheels were mounted. Jason came out of his office to check the rear tyre clearance on the frame: 'Bang on,' he said. 'Phew.'

Periodically, Brian walked by. When Matt got briefly stuck – trying to thread the cables from the new 11-speed Campagnolo levers through the interior of the Cinelli handlebar – the younger mechanics circled round us, half-smirking. With judicious use of a file, a little oil on the cable and some elbow grease, he worked the cables through and the vultures dispersed. Matt then cut the pieces of black cable housing, taking care to ensure the section for the rear brake had the writing centred and reading the right way.

The seat post was cut to length and the Brooks saddle attached: 'Work of art, this one,' Matt said as he clicked the gears up and down, again and again, making micro adjustments, to ensure they were perfectly in sync: 'You must be dead chuffed.'

Actually, I felt rather glum. My journey to put this bike together was at an end. It had been fascinating and great fun. I'd come to realize that the talk about the bicycle being at the dawn of a new golden age was not hyperbole. All the manufacturers I'd spoken to reported growth in the last few years. The balance between craftsmanship and technology is shifting once more, in pursuit of quality. If people want well-made bicycles that are going to last, this shows that the machine is being valued again in a way that it hasn't been for half a century. In Portland, Fairfax, and even in London, I'd witnessed the growth of communities around the bicycle. Bicycles are fashionable – that may not last, but it's indicative of how health concerns, transport issues, the environment and the price of oil are nudging the bicycle back to the centre of public consciousness. In Britain, the establishment are riding bicycles for the first time since the 1890s: to have the Mayor of London, frontbench politicians, national newspaper editors, famous broadcasters such as Jon Snow and Jeremy Paxman and a host of leading businessmen, from the Asda chief executive to fashion guru Paul Smith, not only riding but advocating bicycles would have been unthinkable only twenty years ago.

Bespoke frame-builders are re-adapting the bicycle once again, particularly for urban transportation, with an eye on the future. The world's first cycling magazine, *Le Vélocipède Illustré*, concluded in an editorial in 1869: 'the steel horse fills a gap in modern life,

it is an answer not only to its needs, but also to its aspirations . . .
It's quite certainly here to stay.' The same could be written today.
Twenty years from now, many cities in the developed world will
have successfully re-integrated the bicycle into the transportation
infrastructure. H. G. Wells wrote: 'When I see an adult on a
bicycle, I do not despair for the future of the human race.' He
would have been full of hope today.

I told Matt I was feeling sad that my journey was over. He
looked askance at me. Then he looked at the bike. Then he looked
back at me. He was right. There was a silver lining: a millimetre-
perfect incarnation of one of mankind's greatest inventions. My
dream bike. It was ready.

Brian raised the bike out of the workstand. 'Now then,' he
said, 'jump on here and we'll have a last look at you. Clip in,
relax, grab hold of the brakes there . . . bring this pedal arm down,
dink yer knee back. OK, I'll nick it down a wee bit if you jump
off. And I'll take the saddle back a tad.'

With the saddle adjusted, I climbed back on the bike, supporting myself with an elbow on the workbench. Jason and Matt
stood to one side, looking over the bike with pursed lips, nodding
slowly: a seal of approval.

Brian's eyes and hands moved energetically around the
bike. He stepped back: 'Yer looking good, kid,' he said. 'That's
absolutely the mint.'

In my mind, the first ride was like a TV car advert. I was on an
empty coastal road – Big Sur in California, perhaps, or high above
the Adriatic Sea – barrelling downhill through tight, perfectly
cambered corners. Bike, road and rider were one. The sea spar-
kled. The sun shone. All was Zen.

In reality, I stepped out of my back door in the Black Mountains
to confront a world with no sky. A Welsh poet would have said

the rain was falling softly, like a blessing. Actually, it was just raining. I should have let the rain pass but I couldn't wait. The bike, ready to do battle with all the winds yet unborn, couldn't wait either. You make a covenant with a bike like this – to ride it, and to look after it for as long as it bears you away to a refuge far from the present.

Can a machine have feelings? I recently re-read the diary I had kept while cycling round the world. It confirmed what I suspected then – Mannanan, my bike, never let me down. It never once broke down when I was crossing a desert or a remote mountain range, when I was sick or melancholy or scared of the people I was among. The bike never failed when I was in jeopardy. As soon as we reached a safe haven, and I relaxed, components fell off. In return for this deferral of failure in straitened times, I completely stripped, cleaned and rebuilt the bike every three to six months. I understood how it worked. We were equal partners in a fulfilling journey.

I swung a leg over the bike. Click . . . click . . . into the pedals and we rolled down the lane. Here was the calming familiarity – my window on the world: faster than walking, slower than a train, higher than a car, lower than a plane. The bike felt tight, as you would expect a new, quality bicycle to feel – hard saddle, gears in perfect sync, taut chain and responsive brakes. It felt beautifully balanced, and somehow alive with the hands of the people who had made it.

I dropped down into the Llanthony Valley, commanding the bike through the corners with the tiniest shifts in balance. Briefly, I was going over 35 mph. The bike felt plush and stable. On the long, gentle ascent through the valley, I found a rhythm in the spinning pedals. Rhythm is happiness. A myriad of concerns – about the bike, about this book – dissipated completely. This is the beauty of cycling – the rhythm puts serious activity in the brain to sleep: it creates a void. Random thoughts enter that void – the chorus from a song, a verse of poetry, a detail in the countryside, a joke, the answer to something that vexed me long ago.

Lance Armstrong was wrong. I realize this is rich – telling the winner of the world's toughest cycle race a record seven times that the title of his global, best-selling book, *It's Not About the Bike*, is erroneous – but there you go. I've done it now. Lance, you don't know what you're talking about. It is about the bike. It's *all* about the bike.

Past Capel-y-ffin the road gets steeper. The cloud had peeled back to reveal a canopy of powder blue. The hills shone and the air filled with promise. Climbing out of the saddle, the intensity of effort cast off the last vestiges of ennui. The bike felt eager in my hands.

At Gospel Pass, we slipped through the notch in the rock and the landscape fell away. We began freewheeling slowly downhill. The views into mid-Wales were magnificent. The world lay beyond the handlebars. I was in the best seat in the house: a seat that had cost over $5,500. That's a lot of money for a bicycle, I thought. Then again, it's not a lot of money for the loveliest thing I've ever owned.

Selected Reading

The book that inspired me to cycle round the world was *Full Tilt*, Dervla Murphy's ingenuous account of her intrepid journey by bike from Ireland to India in 1963. It's the best kind of adventure story and a clarion call to 'travel for travel's sake'. I've also read and enjoyed the two-wheel tales of Bernard Magnoloux (*Travels with Rosinante*) and Ian Hibell (*Into the Remote Places*), both of which, in different ways, authentically present the simple pleasures of travelling by bicycle. Tim Moore's *French Revolutions* is a witty introduction to the travails of the Tour de France.

The best autobiographies of time spent 'on the rivet' are written from the thick of it: Paul Kimmage's *Rough Ride* is an exposé of life as a struggling pro, and the drug culture inside the peloton; Matt Seaton's *The Escape Artist* is a heartbreaking tale of love and loss as an amateur racer; *The Flying Scotsman* is the engaging story of Graeme Obree's World Hour Record success; and *One More Kilometre and We're in the Showers* by Tim Hilton is a loving paean to the post-war cycling scene in Britain and Europe. And, of course, there is Lance Armstrong's bullish and best-selling, ghost-written account of recovering from cancer to win the Tour de France, *It's Not About the Bike: My Journey Back to Life*.

Good biographies of great racing cyclists abound: *Major* by Todd Balf gives a good insight into the American pro track scene at the beginning of the twentieth century; *Put Me Back on the Bike* by William Fotheringham perceptively deciphers the enigmatic Tom Simpson. Richard Moore's *In Search of Robert Millar* and

Matt Rendell's *The Death of Marco Pantani* are both finely researched and grippingly written.

Pedalling Revolution by American journalist Jeff Mapes analyses the dynamic of urban cycling culture today. *The Literary Cyclist*, edited by James E. Starrs, is a delightful compendium of excerpts from literature about cycling and cyclists. Surprisingly few novelists have tried to fictionalize the drama of professional cycle racing. Dutch writer Tim Krabbé wrote the excellent and thoughtful *The Rider*; Ralph Hurne's *The Yellow Jersey* will enthral keen cyclists. Other fictional works with cycling or the bicycle central to the narrative include *The Third Policeman* by Flann O'Brien – the story of a love affair between a man and a bicycle, *Three Men on the Bummel* by Jerome K. Jerome and H. G. Wells's *The Wheels of Chance – A Bicycling Idyll*.

The best book I've read about the history of the machine is *Bicycle* by David Herlihy. *King of the Road* by Andrew Ritchie, *Cycling History: Myths and Queries* by Derek Roberts, *On Your Bicycle* by Jim McGurn and *The Story of the Bicycle* by John Woodforde are also very readable. Finally, if you're planning on getting your hands dirty fixing your own bike, *Bicycle Repair* by Rob Van der Plas is a good primer.

Appendix

Useful Information

Tyre size

All tyres have an identification code determined by ETRTO (European Tyre and Rim Technical Organization). It's a universal sizing system that consists of two numbers separated by a dash:

- a two-digit number (the inflated cross-section of the tyre in mm); followed by
- a three-digit number (the diameter of the 'bead seat' of the rim bed in mm).

My Continental Grand Prix 4000 S tyres are: 23–622.

Rim size

Rims also have an ETRTO identification code consisting of two numbers separated by an 'x':

- a three-digit number (the diameter of the 'bead seat' of the rim bed in mm, as with tyres)
- a two-digit number (the inside width of the rim in mm).

My DT Swiss RR 1.2 rims are: 622 x 15.

The critical number is the three-digit number: it must match if the tyres are to fit the rim.

Gear size

How we calculate bicycle gears in the English-speaking world is a curious legacy of the 'high-wheeler' or 'ordinary' bicycle: these machines had no gears and so the 'gear ratio' was simply the diameter of the large front wheel (i.e. the distance covered in one complete revolution of it) given in inches. When the safety bicycle – a machine with a chain drive – was introduced, gearing continued to be calculated with this principle in mind: it still is today, even though it has no physical significance. It is calculated thus:

diameter of the drive wheel (in inches) x the number of teeth on the front chainring ÷ the number of teeth on the rear sprocket = 'gear inches'.

On the Continent, and in countries that use metric measurements, a different gear calculation system called *La developpement* (or 'metres in development') is used. It's more practical as it measures, in metres, the distance the bicycle travels for one crank revolution. It is calculated thus:

number of teeth on the chainring ÷ number of teeth on the rear sprocket x diameter of the wheel (in metres) x pi = 'metres of development' (a number to two decimal points).

Acknowledgements

This book principally owes its existence to two people: my editor at Penguin UK, Helen Conford, who first thought the bicycle deserved a fresh appraisal; and my wife, Vicky, who, knowing I'd always rather be riding than writing, shackled me to a desk while I wrote it.

At Bloomsbury USA, I am immensely grateful to my editor, Pete Beatty, for his enthusiasm and to my publicist, Carrie Majer, for her expertise.

Several people enthusiastically contributed thoughts and ideas: my thanks to Stephen Wood, for arcane stories from the cycling underworld, Victoria Hazael and Chris Juden at CTC, Anna Simms and Matt Davies at Sustrans, John Hudson, Charles Phipps, Roger Crosskey, Joe Christle, Flash, David Miller and Andrew Moore. Brian Palmer, Doug Pinkerton and my old riding buddy, Will Farara, all kindly perused the first draft.

For sharing their love and knowledge of the bicycle, I am grateful to Garrett and Peter Enright at Phil Wood, Chris DiStefano, Diane Chalmers and David Prause at Chris King, Antonio Columbo, Paulo Erzegovesi and Lodovico Pignatti at Cinelli, Lerrj Piazza and Lorenzo Taxis at Campagnolo, Wolf vorm Walde and Hardy Bölts at Continental, Cliff Polton at Royce, Andrea Meneghelli, Steven Green and all the staff at Brooks England, Julian Wall at Cyclefit, Dominic Thomas, Slate Olson, Rudy Contratti, Iacopo Destri, Marco Consonni, Peter Zheutlin, John Moore, Klaus Grüter, Charlie Kelly, Joe Breeze, Billy Savage and Steve 'Gravy' Gravenites. I'm indebted to Chris Anderson for the cover portrait of my dream machine.

For their time and insight into the 'diamond soul', thanks a million to Gary Needham at Argos Cycles, Donald Thomas at Bob Jackson

Cycles, Grant Mosley at Mercian Cycles, Barry Scott at Bespoke Cycling, Chas Roberts at Roberts Cycles, Lee Cooper, Barry Witcomb, Neil Orrell, Paul Corcoran at Pennine Cycles, Vernon Barker, Sacha White at Vanilla, Terry Bill and Keith Noronha at Reynolds Technology and Matt Roberts and all the lads at Rourke Cycles. My greatest debt is to Brian and Jason Rourke.

The dream team at Penguin responsible for putting the book together include Nikki Lee, Rebecca Lee, Jessica Price, Chris Croissant and Mari Yamazaki. I'm delighted to say they all ride. The documentary film based on the book and made for BBC4 drafted a whole new team into the project: thanks to Steve Robinson, Gwenllian Hughes, Emma Haskins, Louis Fonseca and Sally Lisk-Lewis at Indus Films, Ben Hall at Curtis Brown, Steve Bagley at the Coventry Transport Museum, Gwynfor Llewellyn and particularly the producer, Rob Sullivan for showing quenchless enthusiasm for the subject.

My appreciation to Miles, Dawn and Mark in my local bike shop, M & D Cycles, Abergavenny, and to Steve and Cherrie Chadwick, landlord and landlady of my local pub, the Crown at Pantygelli, where much of the first draft was edited. Finally, thank you to my indefatigable agents, Camilla Hornby and Camilla Goslett at Curtis Brown.

Finally, finally, 'aye' to all the friends I've shared so many happy miles with, people who instinctively know that a good bike ride, like life, is about balance: they include Alf Alderson, Chris Anderson, Paulo Baillie, Tommy Bayley, Dave Belton, Rohan Blacker, Harriet Cleverly, James Cole, Tim Doyne, Will Farara, James Greenwood, Tom Halifax, Jimmy Hearn, Simon Martyn, Andy Morley-Hall, Mark Sainsbury, Spencer Skinner, Dave Stirling and Antony Woodward.

Long may you all ride.

Picture Credits

p.vi   Leo Baeck Institute, New York

p.6   Peter Zhleutin

p.8   Robert Penn

p.10   Robert Penn

p.12   Bicycle Books

p.20   Jason/Brian Rourke

p.26   Canada Science and Technology Museum

p.27   Coventry Transport Museum

p.28   Raliegh

p.36   Reynolds

p.40   Historic Hetchins

p.50   Science Museum/SSPL

p.61   Ely Museum

p.69   Robert Penn

p.71   Columbus/Cinelli

p.79   Raleigh

p.91   Renold PLC

p.94   Raleigh

p.95   Campagnolo/Lerrj Piazza

p.98   Campagnolo/Lerrj Piazza

p.114   Robert Penn

p.129   Dewey Livingston

p.131   Charlie Kelly

p.139   Coventry Transport Museum

p.146   The Granger Collection/TopFoto

p.164   *Bicycles & Tricycles: A Classic Treatise on Their Design and Construction* by Archibald Sharp

p.166   Brooks England Ltd

Index

Absolute Hour record, 114
Adams, Sam, 68
Aeolus, 63
'aero bars', 71
A. G. Duckett & Son, 148
Albemarle, Earl of, 144
all-terrain bicycles *see* bicycles;
    mountain
aluminium, 31–2, 34–5, 72–3, 81, 83,
    98, 114, 122
Ambrosio, Giuseppe and Giovani, 72
A Moveable Feast (Hemingway), 162
Anderson, William, 162
Anthony, Susan B., 7
Argos Cycles, 33
Armstrong, Lance, 73, 125, 186
Athlete's Hour record, 114

Bacharach, Burt, 1
Balf, Todd, 160
ball bearings, 60–64, 93
Bartali, Gino, 77–8, 98
Bennett, Charles, 163–4
Benz, Karl, 27
Betjeman, John, 57
Bianchi (Italy), 12, 77, 79, 94, 177
bicycle, the
    diamond frame, 25–9
    dream bike project *see* dream bike
        project
    efficient use of muscle power, 86–90
    frame geometry, 40–43
    history of, *see* history of the bicycle

intrinsic stability, 57
    names for, 112–13
    new golden age, 7
    riding/steering, 55–8, 60, 76–7
    technology borrowed from, 93–5
bicycles
    Ariel, 79, 138–40
    'Breezer', 126, 131, 135
    Chopper, 8, 28
    Cinelli 'Supercorsa', 70
    'clunker', 127–9, 130
    Coventry Machinist, 145
    Dawes roadster, 9
    'Draisine' machines, 48–50, 87–8,
        112
    Hetchins, 33, 39–40
    high-wheeler, 26, 52–4, 112, 139,
        142–6, 157
    Magnum Opus II, 39
    Mannanan, 10, 115, 185
    mountain, 9–10, 60, 81, 110–11,
        126–36, 145, 165
    Nulli Secundus, 39
    Raleigh Hustler, 8–9
    Raleigh Tomahawk, 8, 28, 165
    Safety, 2, 5, 6, 25–8, 54, 57, 77,
        93–4, 100, 101, 110, 116–17,
        146, 149
    Salvo quadricycle, 143
    Saracen Sahara, 9
    Schwinn, 10, 111, 127, 130, 165
    Specialized Rockhopper, 10
    Trivector, 87

bicycles (*cont.*)
   Velocimano tricycle, 88
   velocipedes, 50–52, 88–90, 116, 138
   Viking, 9
   Wilier, 10, 23, 77
Bicycle Union, 157
Bicycling Science, 54
Bidlake, Frederick Thomas, 78
Bike Jockey Strap, 163–4
Boardman, Chris, 113–14
Bob Jackson Cycles, 22
Bolts, Hardy, 115, 117–18, 120–21
Bonds, Alan, 128–9
'boneshakers' *see* bicycles; velocipedes
Bown, William, 63
Breeze, Joe, 110–1, 126, 128–9,
   130–31, 133–5
Brian Rourke Cycles, 19, 22
Brianza, Gaetano, 87
Bridge Pedal event, 68
British Touring Club *see* Cyclists'
   Touring Club
Brooks, John Boultbee, 167
Brooks saddles, 167–74
   B 17 saddle, 167–9, 171, 174
   Team Professional saddle, 173–4
Brown, Sheldon, 29
Bruyneel, Johan, 125
bush roller chains *see* roller chains
Butch Cassidy and the Sundance Kid
   (film), 1

Cambio Corsa ('race changer'
   derailleur), 98
Campagnolo, 77, 95–99, 103–5
   Record groupsets, 104–5, 182
Campagnolo, Tullio, 95–6, 98–99
Campagnolo, Valentino, 97, 103
Cann, Bill, 157
carbon fibre, 32–3, 37, 73–5, 81, 83
carpal tunnel syndrome, 82
'Carve' model (Columbus), 75–6
Cavendish, Mark, 120

Chalmers, Diane, 66
Chris King Precision Components,
   58–60, 64–70
Cinelli, 70–73, 77, 79–81, 83
   1 A handlebar stem, 73
   Spinaci bar extensions, 80
Cinelli, Cino, 70–73, 83, 103
Clausewitz, Carl von, 48
Codex Atlanticus (da Vinci), 100–102
Colombo, Angelo Luigi, 73–75, 77,
   79–83, 182
Columbia Bicycles, 3, 52, 94, 97, 144–5
Columbus tubing, 36, 73–5, 77
Complete Cyclist, The (Pemberton), 54
Continental (tyres), 115–16, 117–18,
   120–21
Contratti, Rudy, 123–4
Cooke, Nicole, 20, 113, 136
Cooper, Edward Ward, 138
Coppi, Fausto, 72, 77, 99, 177
Corcoran, Paul, 21
Cordang, Mathieu, 4
Crane, Stephen, 5
Cycle, The (magazine), 3
Cyclists' Touring Club, 144, 157

da Vinci, Leonardo, 60, 100–103
Denny, Jack, 39–40
derailleurs, 98, 104
Desgranges, Henri, 98
DiStefano, Chris, 58–60, 65–6, 69–70
Drais de Sauerbronn, Baron Karl von,
   48–9, 55, 90, 100
drivetrains, 87, 90, 100, 104, 117, 182
DT Swiss, 122–3, 126
Duchamp, Marcel, 151
Duncan, H. O., 63
Dunlop, John Boyd, 116–17, 120
Dunlop tyres, 116–17

Fairfax, 109, 111, 123–4, 128–9, 183
Fairfax Cyclery, 111
Falconer, Ion Keith, 145

Fischer, Friedrich, 63–4
Fisher, Gary, 128–30
Ford, Henry, 94
Ford Motors, 94
fork rake, 76–7, 127
freewheel clutch, 91

Galsworthy, John, 5
gear size, 190
General Motors, 94
Giro d'Italia race, 72, 83, 99, 105
Goldman, William, 1–2
Gompertz, Lewis, 87
Good Roads Movement, 145
Goodyear, Charles, 120
Goullet, Alf, 160
Gran Premio della Vittoria race, 95
Grand Velocipede Academy, 51
Gravenites, Nick, 124
Gravenites, Steve 'Gravy', 109–15, 121–
    6, 136, 142, 147–53, 182
Great Bicycle Expedition (Anderson), 162
Green, Steven, 170–4, 182
gruppo (groupsets), 103–4
Gymnaclidium *see* Grand Velocipede
    Academy

Hinault, Bernard, 166
handlebars, 57–8, 71–3, 81–3
headsets, 58–60, 64–5, 69–70
head tube angles, 42
Hemingway, Ernest, 30, 155, 161–2
Hercules Cycle and Motor Company
    Ltd, 170
Herlihy, David, 88
Hetchin, Hyman, 39–40
Hillman, William, 94, 139, 142
Hilton, Tim, 12
history, of the bicycle
    chain drives to safety bicycles, 92–6
    da Vinci myth, 100–103
    Draisine to high-wheeler, 47–55
    first golden age, 1–7

genius of James Starley, 137–9
mountain bike history, 110–11,
    127–36
origin of name, 112–13
pneumatic tyre origins, 116–17,
    119–20
saddles, 167–70
use of ball bearings, 60–64
wheels, 140–47
Holbein, Monty, 4
Hughes, Joseph, 63
Hugo, Victor, 2

International Cycling History
    Conference, 100
Irish Cyclist magazine, 116
Italian bicycle industry, 77–9
It's Not About the Bike (Armstrong),
    186
Ixion magazine, 51

Jerome, Jerome K., 54, 162–4
J. K. Starley & Co, 26–7
Johnson, Denis, 50

Keats, John, 49
Kelly, Charlie, 110–11, 128–36
Khunjerab Pass, 85–6
King, Chris, 59
Korbach, 115–16

La Petite Reine, 12
Lallement, Pierre, 87–90, 101
Laumaille, Albert, 145
Lawson, H. J., 91
Le Vélocipède Illustré (magazine), 63,
    183–4
League of American Wheelmen, 145
LeMond, Greg, 37, 166
Leoni, Pompeo, 102
Lessing, Hans-Erhard, 102
London, Jack, 9
Londonderry, Annie, 6

Longabaugh, Harry, 2

McAdam, John, 143
MacMillan, Kirkpatrick, 101
Madison Square Garden, 159–61
Mapplebeck, Johnny, 21–2
maraging steel, 37
Marinoni, Augusto, 101–3
massed-start road racing, 78
Mavic (component company), 98
Mayall, John, 51
Mercian Cycles, 22
Merckx, Eddie, 19, 37, 81, 99, 103, 178
Michaux et Compagnie, 50, 63, 88
Michaux, Pierre, 88, 89
Michelin, André, 120
Michelin, Edouard, 119–20
Michelin tyres, 120
Miller, Charlie, 160
molecular layer interneurons, 56–7
Moore, James, 61–3, 139
Mosley, Grant, 22
Mount Tambora volcano, 47
Murphy, Charles, 4

National Union of Cyclists, 144
Newman, Paul, 1
Nivachrome steel tubing, 74

O'Brien, Flann, 169
offset *see* fork rake
oil crisis 1974, 13, 101, 110
Olivier brothers, 63, 88, 89
*One More Kilometre and We're in the
    Showers* (Hilton), 12
'ordinary' bicycle *see* bicycles; high-
    wheeler
Oregon, 67–8
Orrell, Neil, 21

Paris–Brest–Paris race, 62, 120, 158–9
Paris–Rouen race, 61–3
Parker, Robert LeRoy, 2

Pearsall brothers, 51
Pemberton, A. C., 54
Penn, John, 138
Pennine Cycles, 21
Pneumatic tyres, 116–19
Polton, Clitt, 113–14
Pope, Albert A., 97, 144
Portland, 67–9

quick-release skewers, 96
Quinn, Harry, 20

Raindrops Keep Fallin' on My Head
    (Bacharach), 1
Raleigh Bicycle Company, 12–13, 28,
    94
Renold, Hans, 91–4
Repack (off-road trail), 110–11, 126,
    128–35
Reynolds, 36–8, 74
    '531' steel alloy tubing, 37
    '953' steel alloy tubing, 37–9, 44
Reynolds, Alfred Milward, 36
Reynolds, Tessie, 6
riding schools, 49–52
Ritchey, Tom, 128, 130, 152
Ritchie, Andrew, 137
Roberts, Chas, 35
Roberts Cycles, 10, 35
Roberts, Matt, 182–4
roller chains, 91–4
Rourke, Brian, 19–21, 22–6, 29–30,
    42–43, 75–6, 82, 104, 113,
    177–82, 184
Rourke, Jason, 22, 24, 38–41, 43–5,
    178–82, 184
Rover Cycle Company, 27
Royce hubs, 113–15, 126
running machine (Baron von Drais), 100

Sapim, 124–6
Schütz, Horst, 156–7, 162
Scientific American (periodical), 51

'seat cluster', 45
seat tube angles, 42
Selle Italia, 166
Selle San Marco, 165–6
Sharp & Smith, 164
Shelley, Mary, 47
Simpson, Tommy, 19–20, 62, 156–7
Sivrac, Comte de, 100
six-day races, 157–62
Smith, Robert A., 6
Stanley bicycle show 1895, 3
Starley, James, 79, 93, 137–9, 142–3, 147, 152
Starley, John Kemp, 26–9, 94, 110, 163
steel, 15, 31, 33–9, 72–5, 126, 183
Stevens, Thomas, 145
Streuvels, Stijn, 113
suffragettes, 6
Sun Also Rises, The (Hemingway), 155–6
Suriray, Jules Pierre, 63

Taming the Bicycle (Twain), 52–4
Taxis, Lorenzo, 95, 103, 105
Taylor, Jack, 20
Taylor, Major, 160
Telford, Thomas, 143
Terront, Charles, 120, 158–9
Third Policeman, The (O'Brien), 169
Thomas, B. J., 1
Thomas, Donald, 22
Thomson, Stu, 133
Three Men on the Bummel (Jerome), 162–3
thrust stress, 60
TIG/MIG welding processes, 39, 43
time trials, 78
titanium, 31, 34, 37, 114
Tolstoy, Leo, 54

Tour de France race, 4, 19, 37, 42, 62, 77–8, 98–9, 103, 105, 120, 159, 160, 166 177
'trail', 76
tubular tyres, 120
Turner, J. M. W., 47
Turner, Josiah, 138
Twain, Mark, 52–5
tyre size, 189

Unicanitor, 70
Varied Radius Concept, 82
Vaughn, Philip, 63
Vélo, 113
velocinasiums, 51
vertical integration, 94
Vigorelli velodrome, 80, 103
vulcanization, 120–21

Waller, George, 158
Wells, H. G., 5, 55, 184
Wheaton, C., 145
Wheelman, The (magazine), 144
wheels
    history, 140–41
    lever-tension, 140–42
    rims, 121–3, 189
    spokes, 124–6, 135–7, 147–53, 191
    tangent-spoked, 142–3, 147
Wheels of Chance, The (Wells), 5
White, Sacha, 69
Wild Bunch, the, 2
Witcomb Cycles, 13
'Wrapover' seat stay, 45
Wright Cycle Company, 95
Wright Flyer, 27, 95–6
Wright, Wilbur and Orville, 27, 95–6

Zimmerman, Arthur A., 4
Zinn, Lennard, 10